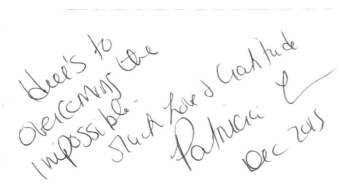

The Missing Piece in Forgiveness

Overcoming the Impossible

Compiled By Kate Gardner

Introduction

I sat on my bed looking down at the 3rd Missing Piece book manuscript feeling quite sad. I didn't want this to be the last 'Missing Piece' book and I didn't want to stop placing amazing stories out to the world.

'The Missing Piece,' book series has touched hundreds of lives across the world. Not just of the readers who bought the books, but also the lives of all the authors within the books. This has been one complete life changing journey for each and for all the people who came in to contact with these books.

Why End a Great Thing?

There it was again, that voice popped up inside of me, just like it had done at the beginning of my self-discovery journey, telling me loud and clear an instruction that was about to change my life and take me on an incredible journey once again. I made the decision right there and then that this was far from the end!

In fact this was the beginning! I started shaking with nerves and my teeth started chattering once more. Chattering just like they had the day I sat at my laptop and signed up to Jack Canfield's coaching program two and half years ago. I went downstairs and told my partner Matthew of my plans. Oh no! That was it, I had said it out loud, which means I had just asked the universe for what I truly wanted. Within a matter of days the 'how' started to show up. I got scared for a few weeks and started to resist. Like all human beings, I rejected something I was scared of, which led to me needing bed rest for two days with a lovely sore throat to go with it.

When you resist something your body will show signs of weakness from you fighting against energy that is too powerful to defeat. You just make yourself sick trying and then your ego tramples its heels into the back of your sub-conscious mind with its toxic comments and put downs; "You will never make this work", "What makes you think you are good enough to make this succeed?".

For two days, I laid there resting and bombarding my mind with positive information and reading positive mind-set books. By Monday morning I got out of bed looked in the mirror and said to the reflection, "You are going to do this and you are going to succeed. Now get your shit together and be the leader you were born to be."

I sat at my desk that morning and announced live over my podcast show that, 'The Missing Piece', was far from finished. I also made the announcement to the world that there would not just be a forth book, but a never ending series with people invited from all over the world to have their own books too.

That day, 'The Missing Piece Publishing House', was born and here is the 4th book in your hands right now. Each book you read means more to me than the one before it because it is another leg of the journey. It shows you how far we have actually come. The whole, 'Missing Piece,' journey started from myself experiencing domestic violence and my own daughter being raped. It came from the burning passions of a mother's love, which continue to burn bright inside me every single day.

This is more than just a book series to me; it's a big huge part of mine and Emily's life. Through the power of these books and mentoring, we survived our own traumas and helped other people get through theirs. Emily wrote her story in the last book and set herself free from the trauma she experienced nearly four years ago. To be young and set free already means she now has the rest of her life to live without guilt, shame, or bad feelings lurking in the back of her mind.

She has now moved on and forgiven herself and forgiven those who hurt her at the time, which is why the subject for this book is forgiveness. Forgiveness is not a pardon to someone to let them think they have gotten away with what they did to you. Forgiveness is a blessing to help you release yourself from an emotional prison of bitter feelings that otherwise would consume you and make your life less happy.

I now invite you into the 4th book of, 'The Missing Piece,' book series, where you can read stories from amazing people all across the world who have come together to share their experiences and you will read how the power of forgiveness truly set them free.

Welcome to Freedom
Welcome to Inspiration
Welcome to 'The Missing Piece in Forgiveness: Overcoming the Impossible'

With Love & Gratitude

Kate Gardner
#1 International Best-Selling Author & CEO of
The Missing Piece Publishing House
www.themissingpiecebooks.com

Kate Gardner

Kate Gardner is a #1 International Best-Selling Author/Podcast Host/International Success Coach & CEO of The Missing Piece Publishing House.

As a Success Coach, Kate informs, motivates and empowers online business owners, and helps provide them with the business tools and skills they need to succeed in their online businesses. Kate helps raise her clients' self-esteem and self-confidence through providing tools to change their mind-set, so they are prepared for the responsibility that success brings to them.

As a publisher, Kate is the creator of the International Best Selling Book Series,' The Missing Piece,' which provides a platform for authors and online business owners to grow their network, with every intention of making them a best-selling author.

Kate's ultimate goal is to help you build a successful international platform and succeed in turning your following into raving fans that constantly buy from you.

You can reach Kate at:

Website: www.themissingpiecebooks.com

Website: www.kate-gardner.co.uk

Playing the Blame Game Leads to You Losing

By Kate Gardner

My first reaction was that I wanted to hunt him down and punch him right in the face. I was angry and I wanted him to suffer as much as my child did. The past 18 years of my life I spent protecting, loving, and respecting both of my children. I had amazing relationships with both of them and they lived in an environment where being completely honest and open about their feelings was accepted.

Now here I was, knelt on my knees outside my daughter's bedroom door, begging her to let me in. The pain of seeing her having an emotional and mental breakdown at the age of fourteen was killing me. I felt completely useless, annoyed, and angry that someone I didn't know was having this effect on me and my child. I started banging my fists up against the door begging for her to let me in, just so I could hold her and tell her that everything was going to be alright, and no matter what, we would get through this together.

My palms slid down the side of the door as I wept. I lay outside her door curled up in ball feeling excruciating, emotional pain. Not only had the person who raped my daughter taken away her innocence and emotional stability, he had also crushed what I had worked so hard to create all those years up to this point.

There were many weeks of conversations through the door, leaving her dinner outside on the landing, and slipping notes of love under her door. Finally, one day she opened her bedroom door and fell into my arms and cried until she couldn't cry any more. She trusted me enough again to realise I only wanted to love and protect her.

I may have had my daughter back in my arms again, but I still felt bitterness deep inside of me. It was a feeling of being robbed, like somebody had taken something away from me so dear and important, which they had! He took my innocent little girl without permission and I was bitter. I also had to mourn the loss of a child that I would never know to be my Emily again, the one that didn't have a care in the world had gone for good.

I didn't think it could get much worse, but it did. Emily's rapist moved on to the same road as our house. All the work I had placed into her to try and get her to open up and trust me had completely disappeared; we were back at square one.

Emily started suffering from anxiety and she would experience a panic attack when it came to walking past her rapist's house. He added to this mental torture by hanging out his bedroom window and shouting at her. He would tell her that she had deserved what he had done to her, leaving Emily to run home in more floods of tears and hide away from the world more. I was annoyed and really wanted to go over there and bang on his door and give him a piece of my mind. Only my hands were completely tied due to the legal battle that we started to have him convicted. You don't want to know how many times I fantasied about punching him! I am not a violent person, but boy did I want to kick his butt and throttle him. One day I passed him when walking down the street. It was only a two second encounter, but it changed the way I thought about him and a lot of things in this world.

You see that day, Emily was by my side. When she saw her rapist coming towards us, she started to panic, even more so because he was not alone. He was walking towards us both with his mother at his side.

As we passed both of them in the street, his mother glared at Emily and gave her the dirtiest look, the kind of look that would turn milk sour if it was possible. Seeing the woman's face screw up like that was an awakening moment for me. It made me realise that he possible couldn't know any better if he had been brought up by someone else refusing to take responsibility.

He was only the way he was because the environment he had grown up in was not a fantastic one. His mother had allowed him to have girls as young as 12 years old in the house. Not only that, but also in his room! What he was doing was normal practice because no boundaries had been set by his mother to begin with. Now that glare she was giving my daughter in the street was her rejecting her responsibilities and looking outside herself for somebody else to blame, rather than taking it on the chin and accepting her wrong parenting skills had resulted to this.

It was then that my bitterness and anger went. I sat Emily down that evening and explained my awakening to her and she completely understood it too. How could anybody in life be expected to live up to a high standard we expected when the person who is supposed to guide them provides very little stability for them in the first place? All they knew was how to not take responsibility for their actions and blame everybody else for their wrong doing.

This was a huge breakthrough for Emily and me to move forward. It also gave Emily the incentive to write her story in full view on the Freedom & Empowerment campaign page in front of 4,500 people. Emily had the strength to go one step further and publish her story in, 'The Missing Piece: a Life Transformed.' Each time Emily shared her story, she was gaining back her freedom and realising her guilt and bitterness that had haunted her at the beginning. She learned to trust again and even fell in love for the first time.

Further down the journey, I let go and forgave Emily's rapist and his mother's reaction to my daughter. Seeing my daughter light up and be free and in love was a delight to see after the hell we had been through. Over the next two years, Emily grew into an amazing young woman and the time came for her to fly the nest with her partner into their own apartment.

We have come a long way over the past four years, to see the light at the end of the tunnel. Emily's journey gave me the incentive to start a domestic violence campaign page on Facebook to support other victims of domestic violence and rape. In only two and a half short years, our passion continued to burn and we soon turned that campaign page in to an International Best-selling book series and a publishing house. When testing times are sent to you and the emotional pain is raw, I want you to consider how sharing your experience can make you stronger and touch lives on a daily basis.

People will look towards you as a beacon of light shining on them and your words will give them hope so that they can move forward from their pain. For myself to have come this far, I contribute wholeheartedly to forgiveness; not just forgiveness of those who had hurt me in the past, or Emily's rapist, but to forgive myself too for feeling the bittiness and the shame because that alone was keeping me stuck.

When I forgave, I set myself free and moved forward with my life. It helped my daughter move forward with hers also, so much so that next year I will be a grandmother.

Emily is expecting her first child this year. I gained a bright amazing young woman, a global movement, and another generation to inspire.

Forgiveness is the key to freedom and you are the master of that key.

April M. Lewis

April M. Lewis is a passionate health communicator committed to making healthy living achievable for everyone. Combining years of being an athlete, student, leader, and professional, she has developed practical approaches anyone can use to have a well-balanced mind, body, and spirit. After years of teachings from great masterminds, she accepted her calling and began her journey to spread the good news about health. She is committed to living a healthy life and motivating and inspiring others to do the same. April is a U. S. Army veteran and a native of Mobile, AL.

You can reach April at:

Website: www.IAmAprilLewis.com

Facebook: www.facebook.com/exposethetruth1

Life after Death
By April M. Lewis

"This can't be happening. No. Are you serious? No. Oh my God. No. Please God, no." Those words were the only ones I could get out of my mouth. I could not believe what I just heard, it couldn't be real. Moments before those repetitive words of disbelief, I received a phone call that would forever change my life. It was February 27, 2006. Not only was this phone call a complete break of the United States Army policy, it was a call that began my spiral down the deepest, darkest hole of my life. A cracking voice on the other end of the phone struggled to say, "April, your husband was killed." I sat straight up. I could only say, "No. How? What?" The voice continued, "I am sorry, I know I am not supposed to be calling, but I couldn't let you find out another way." I literally felt my heart stop beating. A voice next to me said, "What's wrong?" Tears were rolling down my face and as I gasped for air I said, "My husband was just killed." I was in bed with another man when my husband was killed in Iraq.

It is painful to read, painful to write, and it was even more painful to live. Nevertheless, I am thankful I am able to share my story. I lived almost nine years holding on to the guilt and shame that almost ended my life on several occasions. The best thing that could have happened to me was meeting, loving, and marrying Dwayne Lewis. The second best thing that could have happened to me was learning how to forgive myself – even as a sinner.

Who would have thought a short drive to Wendy's one evening would be where our relationship would begin? He asked if I was single; I was, and the rest is beautiful history. Dwayne and I fit into each other's lives like a glove. We dated one year before we were married. In that year, I experienced unconditional love and what connecting with your soulmate felt like. Some people will go their entire life and never be able to say the same, we were so blessed and everything was perfect, until it wasn't.

In 2001, I received orders to Germany, which hurt our relationship. He was afraid he was going to lose me and I felt the same. He proposed breaking up and I told him that wasn't an option. We had our first fight. We were young, in love, and didn't know what to do. It only became harder when his life-long dream of being an Infantryman became a reality. In a matter of weeks everything changed.

We married in 2003, just months before Dwayne's first deployment to Afghanistan. This is when the road became rocky and I lost my footing. Prior to his deployment, thousands of miles apart, we managed to talk every day. When he was deployed that all changed. Dwayne left and I didn't hear anything from him in months. I was confused. Was he alive? Did he still love me? I reached out and got nothing in return. I was embarrassed. I was married, but didn't have a clue as to where my husband was. I remember thinking I was such a fool for hoping our marriage would be any different from the other shattered military marriages. I went to my leadership for help.

One morning I opened my inbox and saw an email from him. I screamed, "DWAYNE!" I was so excited! That was until I read it. He was mad. He was mad that I reached out looking for him. He assumed that I knew of his current conditions and contacting me wasn't priority. I honestly didn't know that, which was why I reached out in the first place. I was crushed; I felt like my heart had been ripped out and thrown against the wall. He acted as if I really knew war – I hadn't deployed yet – nor was I prepared to not hear anything from him. This is where I lost my footing. I went to my room, laid his picture facedown and said, "Fuck love". This isn't what I thought love was and I didn't want the pain. That moment led to a rough next few years. I should have never said those words.

Dwayne and I reconnected and it was not the same. Or at least, I didn't think so. How could someone who I wanted to be my forever hold such a hurtful place in my life? I went numb. That was until that call came through on 2-27-06. I recently heard you grieve as hard as you love, that explains the past nine years.

What had I done? We spoke the same vows, "Until death do us part." Did I follow through? I hated myself.

"God, why wouldn't you let me make it right? People get mad all the time and no one ends up dead. Why would you let this happen to me?" I hated God.

"Why did you just forget about me? I was scared too. We said forever. You know I was a spoiled brat. You should have just called." I hated Dwayne.

After 2-27-06, my life was completely in God's hands because I mentally checked-out. I went through the motions of work and school, but I was the walking dead. I became a functioning addict. My motto was, "One Life, Why Not." I would tell myself you only get one life then we end up in a box, so why not do what we want? I was now stationed at Ft. Bragg and only a few of my amazing friends witnessed and protected me in this dark time. I would have nervous breakdowns and become violent. I couldn't sleep with my back to the door for years. I would feel Dwayne's presence, but be terrified. I would swallow pills with alcohol just to sleep. I lost my mind. One night, I sat on the side of my bed and thought if I just killed myself I wouldn't feel anything anymore.

Holding that thought, I finally felt relief. I welcomed death. That's when I knew I needed to move and start my life over.

I moved to South Carolina and began my healing process. I began working with my life coach who taught me to meditate. This practice allowed me to hear Dwayne's voice clearly say he forgave me and he loved me. I truly felt his forgiveness. I knew in my heart that my husband was still my husband, I only walked away. Dwayne's best friend, who was there throughout it all, reassured me of his love when I was at my lowest point.

I also got connected to my spiritual family. I learned that we serve a forgiving God and I couldn't do anything to take His love away. God forgave me.

One night at my neighbor's house, I had a complete breakdown. I wanted to give-up on life, again. I was going to move away, but this time I wasn't going to tell anyone. I didn't feel like I deserved anything. It had been six years of suffering and my heart hardened like never before. Sitting on her ottoman, I suddenly became very cold. Dwayne whispered in my right ear, "Look at the clock." I didn't have on my glasses so I asked her what time it was. It was 11:11. I burst in to tears and dropped my head. She was completely freaked out. He said, "Look up." I looked straight up at a candle she was burning and he said, "This is the fire that burns forever. Our love will burn forever."

The picture I placed facedown when I said, "Fuck love", was a picture of him at dinner. During this dinner, Dwayne put a candle in the centre of the table and said the fire represented our love. He told me our love was like an eternal flame that would never burn out.

It never did.

Love covers a multitude of sin and the love we had covered my sin. I forgave myself.

It took years of guilt, shame, grief, and silence to get to this place of freedom. I had to forgive myself because everyone else in the equation had forgiven me. I was choosing to self-sabotage because of my actions and I lost eight years of my life. I sustained because I focused on my health and exercise; it was my release. In 2014, I realized that I am completely at peace in the gym, his favorite place.

We all sin and fall short of the glory of God. We do it countless times and we will until we take our last breathe. His grace and mercy will cover us if we allow it. Be honest with yourself. Forgive those who have hurt you. Forgive yourself. We do not know what tomorrow will bring so embrace each day as if it truly is the last. Forgiveness is the only way to overcome the impossible.

Aurora Wilson

Aurora Wilson is the founder of, 'Verite' International', a healthcare management company and is also the founder of, 'Aurora Wilson Ministries.' She is the co-founder of, 'iCoach & Co', where she is a Spiritual, Wellness, and Business Coach. Aurora is also the co-founder of, 'The Christian Speakers Women Movement.' She is a member of several professional organizations, a licensed and ordained minister, inspirational speaker, and International Best-selling Author. She is an administrator with, 'I Am A Ruby Ministry School.' Aurora believes in helping people to, "Reignite Your Internal Light", by helping individuals heal the mind and the body.

You can reach Aurora at:

Telephone: 770-8-AURORA (770-828-7672) & 888-899-2767 ext. 703

Email: aurora@aurorawilson.com

Website: www.aurorawilson.com

Website: www.icoachco.com

Facebook: www.facebook.com/AuroraWilson

Twitter: www.twitter.com/msaurorawilson

LinkedIn: www.linkedin.com/in/aurorawilson

Church Hurt and Forgiveness
By Pastor Aurora Wilson

Life is not always a pleasant walk down the garden path. Who has not known pain and anguish? Have you experienced a life situation where you felt like your spiritual beliefs were tested and may have asked yourself, "Why God is this happening to me?" Or, "Where are you God when I need you?" Have you sought comfort and refuge, advice and support from a spiritual leader or someone you trusted for spiritual guidance, wisdom and they ended up hurting you? Well I have and when you've been hurt by someone you entrusted with your spiritual health the un-forgiveness, hurt, or betrayal you may feel can haunt your mind every day, unless you learn to forgive them and yourself.

Many times in life when we have been disappointed, feel lonely, abandoned, mistreated, hurt, neglected, not loved, talked about, been through a failed relationship, financial setback, difficulty with raising children, dealing with grief, job loss, and even rejected by family or friends, we search for a way to heal, forgive, and find the peace we desire. We start by getting in tune with our spiritual side, our intuition, and our inner being.

We start looking for solutions to our problems and seek a way to channel our negative energy in order to release positive energy. Some may meditate, join organizations, attend a local place of worship, or find a place of Zen at home, etc. We seek out these various channels to connect with ourselves and with others who can positively help us overcome our negative feelings.

I was at this place in life a few years ago. After my divorce, deteriorating health, loss of income, business failure, and death of my son, I needed someone to talk to. I wanted to find a person who I felt would understand my situation and give me the support and comfort I was in need of. One morning I decided to return to a place of worship. I had not attended an organize place of worship in years, but I felt like my back was against the wall and I needed to see someone; I was falling down a dark path fast by wanting to commit suicide and I was deeply depressed every day.

I sought help from a spiritual organization seeking prayer and guidance. Instead what happened was people started gossiping, spreading my business, judging me, and I was victimized by a male in the organization. My experience with these people made me feel like I was a terrible person and I that must have done something wrong and God was punishing me and they questioned my beliefs.

I became bitter and angry with what happened. Instead of expressing how I felt, I held it in and I allowed this anger to replay in mind over and over like a scratched record. I became so angry that I started cursing God and cursing people who were pretending to follow their faith. I started telling others I didn't believe in God and the people at church were not positive. What I was dealing with was un-forgiveness.

For years, I found myself in a constant struggle and battle with my own thoughts. I stayed away from anything that mentioned the words, "spirituality", "church", or "positive thinking". I said, "Who is this God? A God who will allow me to hurt, a God who will take my son, a God who will allow my marriage to fail?" I went on and on. I had so much un-forgiveness in my heart and refused to try and forgive people in my mind.

One day I met someone who said, "Aurora, forgiveness is not about saying they are right, it is about releasing yourself so you can heal and move on. It is about letting go of those things you can't control. Stop looking to humans for your answers and internal happiness and listen to the small still voice inside you, your intuition that will not lead you astray." I began to mediate, pray, and find a place of Zen. The goal is to go back to the person who was hurt and saying, "I am healed, I forgive, I let go of things, and I release the pain so that I can heal."

In time, I found that I was healed and I was able to forgive those who hurt me. No longer did I run from church, spiritual leaders, or others, but I embraced who I am and who loves me, and that is God. I began on a journey of forgiving them and myself.

"Reignite their internal light, which life has tried to extinguish".

By not forgiving, you have chosen to shackle yourself like a prisoner to your past! This holds you back from experiencing your true Divine Potential. You carry the great weight of shame upon your shoulders and the burdens upon your back. The grudges and revenge wreak havoc in your mind and the ball chained to your leg impedes your forward growth. You hold the power and one of the keys that can potentially heal you, ultimately setting you free!

When we carry grudges, resentments, and old hurt and pains, we end up hurting ourselves more than the ones that we perceived did the hurting! Being unforgiving is detrimental to our entire being!

Forgive what needs to be forgiven. Forgiveness can be liberating.

Inevitably in life, we will face disapproval or rejection from others. Remind yourself that you may encounter people who will hurt you, and yes that person may be an inspirational leader, counsellor, spiritual leader, or leader at a local ministry. You may have sought the guidance, wisdom, and support from a spiritual advisor and they have hurt you more than help you, but know that it is okay. Your intuition and that small inner voice will speak to you and tell you what to do and who to do it with. Ask yourself, "Are you listening to the voice?"

Sometimes we focus on a person, not God. We think the person should have no faults. We may put them on a pedestal and become disappointed when they hurt us.

Forgiveness has to be given without resentment and in honesty. It must be completely genuine or else it is not truly forgiven. You are only fooling yourself if you do not forgive from the heart. What if the person we are forgiving does not feel that they have done anything wrong? It doesn't matter; forgive them anyways. If the other person involved chooses not to accept responsibility that is ok. Self-empowerment is taking care and doing things for you. You do not need their permission or approval for you to heal or to forgive them! You owe this to yourself. You are only responsible for your own healing. In truth, when you do forgive the other person, a higher part of this being knows and accepts your forgiveness.

What I learned from my personal experience and tips for you:

Take Your Power Back.

A very powerful way to set you free with forgiveness is through energy work, meditations, and visualizations that work specifically to de-program your subconscious mind.

Go into your physical sacred space, sit and start a list.

Write down every single name that you seek or hear that you feel has created any type of hurt, pain, or suffering. Write down each name without judgment.

When you feel your list is complete, go back again, and this time write down all the names that you feel you have hurt either intentionally or unintentionally.

After you are done, go through the list and for each person say, "I forgive (name) and I forgive myself now. I release all karmic energy that we have together in all directions of time. I send you love and bless you on your way. I call upon the power of God to cut any and all spiritual cords between myself and (name) now. These spiritual cords are now lovingly severed, lifted, loved, healed, released, and let go. I therefore accept fully and completely the healing of my relationship with (name) now. Thank you! So be it and so it is!"

This does take a while, but it is very powerful. Free yourself and move on!

Remember

Forgiveness is about creating a state of forgiving both to self and others. It is excusing a mistake or an offense and letting go of the associated hurt, anger, or resentment because forgiveness has the greatest benefit to the person doing the forgiving; it is one of the greatest gifts that you can give to yourself.

I hope my story has inspired you. I encourage you to reach out to me for a free 30- minute Soul Renewal consultation session by visiting: http://www.vcita.com/v/workwithaurora

Bernadette Bingham

The second oldest of 14 children, Bernadette grew up on a farm near Saginaw Michigan. Married to her soul mate for 42 years, she has two daughters, two sons in love, and 7 amazing grandchildren.

Currently Vice President of the Saginaw County Chamber of Commerce, Bernadette has written articles that have been published in Chamber of Commerce publications and has been a key speaker at state-wide leadership conferences, retreats, and other events.

She enjoys preparing and facilitating women's growth and inner healing groups, and spiritually mentoring women.

You can reach Bernadette at:

Email: bernibingham@gmail.com

Phone: (989) 835 6160

Harden Not Your Heart
By Bernadette Bingham

Forgiveness, for me, is a journey that is sometimes three steps forward, sometimes two steps back. It's a process that I often have to work at as I peel the layers away and find out what's really going on with me and why I'm so angry, hurt, or resentful towards others. I don't always find it easy or quick to forgive. Nor do I always want to.

There was a lot of confusion and pain in my life and I never felt I was good enough in the eyes of others. Belonging to a large family, and because I had such a strong sense of responsibility, my relationships with others were often as a caretaker. I felt like I didn't fit in and wasn't valued or approved of unless I was doing something to benefit others. Too busy to develop friendships, I never learned how to have fun. I've always tried to do what was expected of me. Somehow, I thought if I did everything I "should", people would like me and I would be successful and happy; it didn't work.

As I got older, I embraced my religious faith and found comfort in knowing and following my church's rules. I believed that God would approve my dedication and I would then be special to Him, if not to anyone else. Somehow that seemed to work for me until I became a wife and Mother. Married to a wonderful man, with two lovely daughters, I experienced love that was more real, intense, deeper, and complete than I had ever imagined possible.

As the love for my family grew, my heart began to hunger for a deeper connection with God. For years I did all the right things; I prayed, fasted, read scriptures, and participated in church and prayer meetings. I taught catechism, Sunday school, and vacation Bible school. My hunger grew, but my heart seemed unchanged. I didn't understand why I couldn't connect with Him. My own self-esteem and relationships with others remained empty and lonely as well. What was I doing wrong that God seemed farther away than ever? Why couldn't I relate better to the people in my life?

One day, something clicked for me. I began to understand that God really was there. He was like the sun; forever shining, warming, healing, and helping people grow. I also began to understand that my hunger was real. I was reaching out to God with arms opened, but I felt I was constantly living in the shadows; the sun rarely touched me even though it was right there, and I didn't understand why.

Thus began my journey of true growth and forgiveness.

I sought a spiritual director and a therapist. I read inner healing books and joined support groups. The Bible and the AA Big Book became my guides. I kept a journal and I prayed.

I began to have the most painful, yet liberating self-awareness. I understood that between me and God (and others in my life) there was a wall. This was a huge, solid wall of rock that hardened my heart, making it impossible for God's Light and Grace to shine through. Anytime I had resentment against anyone, deserved or not, I picked up a rock and added it to the wall. I cemented it with unforgiveness. I learned that by building this wall, I had shut out not only God, but the people in my life. It was like armor that I thought kept me from being vulnerable and hurt. It just left me isolated and alone.

I began to identify the rocks: Someone hurt my feelings (add a medium sized stone of self-pity and resentment). Someone treated me unfairly (bigger rock of self-pity, resentment, and anger). Someone rejected me or disagreed with me (more rocks and even boulders) and it went on and on. I found that many of the rocks and boulders I carried were without merit. Many had more to do with my misunderstanding or perception, or my own issues, than with reality. I often struggled as I looked at different situations and relationships from my past. I didn't want to accept any responsibility if I misjudged someone's actions or intent. I wanted to justify my resentment and I certainly didn't relish having to ask forgiveness of those I had wronged.

I've learned much wisdom on my journey to understand, ask for, and receive forgiveness: Here are just a few:

- In order to have a more intimate relationship with God, I need to have a more honest and real relationship with the people in my life, including myself.
- Everything isn't about me. If someone does something I don't like or I find hurtful, they might not be doing it to cause me pain. I've learned that if others don't agree with me or they do things differently, it doesn't necessarily mean one of us is right and one is wrong. It might just be two people looking at things in different ways. It could be about them and their own issues.
- It's ok to say no. I was afraid that if I said no, or disagreed with someone, they'd 'throw me away.' (When I started to say, "no", many did.) Just because I can, doesn't mean I should. Learning this was very freeing for me. Everything wasn't my responsibility. If someone asked me to do something, it didn't mean I had to do it. I could say no without being a bad person.
- Just because I'm not loved on my terms, doesn't mean I'm not loved. Misunderstanding this was a cause for boulders

27

of resentment to be placed in my wall. I've come to believe that most people do the best they can with what they have and where they are at.

- I learned that perceptions and feelings are not necessarily facts. When I feel unloved or I think others judge me it doesn't mean they actually do. It became important for me to learn how to identify and compartmentalize feelings and perceptions from facts. If something feels like a big deal to me doesn't mean it's a big deal to someone else.

- Feelings are neither right nor wrong, they just are. I have the right to my feelings. I have a right to process my feelings for the purpose of getting past them. I don't have the right to take my painful feelings out on anyone.

- People respond to different situations in their own way, and that's ok. Even though my heart was breaking, I didn't cry at my Father's funeral because I'm not a crier. I've overhead people say I was cold and didn't care.

- Just because someone blames me doesn't mean it's my fault. Sometimes, maybe it's no one's fault; maybe it just is.

- Win-win is the ideal outcome of all situations. Others don't have to lose for me to win or be wrong for me to be right. We have different perceptions.

- Resentment is like a cancer fed by unforgiveness. The longer it's there and the more I nurture it, the more it grows and destroys my spirit.

- When I'm wrong or I hurt someone, I need to admit I'm wrong and ask forgiveness. Not just of God, but from the person I harmed, without placing blame or making the apology conditional on their willingness to forgive me.

- Forgiving doesn't necessarily mean forgetting or trusting. They are three separate words with three completely different meanings.
- I've learned that forgiveness isn't just about other people, it's about forgiving me.
- When I'm carrying and enjoying resentment and don't want to let it go, I've learned to pray for the person or situation I resent, asking God to bless them and release me of all negativity towards them. When I can't or won't forgive, I pray God will bring me to that place and that I do not harden my heart and rebuild the wall that keeps me in shadows and keeps His Grace and Light, and the love of other people, out.

Certainly, too often, others DO hurt me, wrong me, judge me, or reject me, often times deeply. They may purposely hurt me to the core and enjoy it. Even then, I've learned that I need to forgive, as I want to be forgiven. Currently I have a lot of pain in my life and I struggle. I'm tempted to be bitter and to feel sorry for myself. I'm tempted to be angry and resentful, but, for my own sake, I know my only choice is to forgive and let it go.

I'm learning to be open, to be vulnerable, to accept my and others' humanness, and to embrace life as I continue my Forgiveness Journey.

Debbie McLaren

Debbie McLaren is a three-time Best Selling Author/Speaker/Singer/Songwriter who received Runner-Up Placement in the, '2012 Song of the Year Songwriting Contest.' Debbie has just recently finished recording her song. While taking her music to the next level, her future plans include music/speaking ministry in churches and other venues.

Debbie's day job is working in the Human Services field helping others reach their goals and dreams. By the Grace of God, Debbie has 29 years of sobriety and shares her experience, strength, and hope with others that they too may find freedom!

You can reach Debbie at:

Email: deb.mclaren@shaw.ca

Website: www.debbiemclaren.wix.com/author

Souncloud: www.soundcloud.com/debjmac

MacJams: www.macjams.com/artist/debmac

YouTube: www.youtube.com/user/debbiemclaren

In The Midst of Forgiveness
By Debbie McLaren

Trust was being built, respect was mutual, and misunderstandings were becoming clear. Plans were being made and progress was happening, finally. By all indication of recent events, I thought this was going to be a good thing. What happened next, I didn't see coming. Betrayal at its deepest knocked the wind out of me. I couldn't breathe and felt like I had been punched in the gut. I've experienced betrayal before in different types of relationships, but this one still astounds me.

I think I manoeuvred through the week in shock, doing what I had to do, but not really there. Disbelief for a while, then the anger rose so high it erected a wall to protect my heart. No more getting hurt here! Staying angry would guarantee I wouldn't excuse, give in and reconcile; anger would be my friend for a while.

Even with as much experience with betrayal and forgiveness as I had through the years, I failed to heed my own advice. Knowing that hanging on to anger never really does any good, except, yes stay away from the person that hurt you, I clung to it. In the meantime, it affected every area of my life, patience was nil, and displaced anger toward others happened all too often. I went about apologizing for my abrupt manner and angry tone at times and decided it was time to get on with this business of forgiving. I was not thrilled about this I must say, even though I know that the sooner I forgive the sooner I'm free, but it became so tangled in my whole being, I just couldn't see my way through this one. I believe God works in mysterious ways. That night I watched a video about someone's story on forgiveness, I cried and knew then that I had to forgive this person. With a soft and open heart,

I prayed and asked God to help me forgive this person. I also asked for forgiveness for the mistakes I made along the way and for the hurt I may have caused in the process. Then, I had to forgive myself. It seemed easy at that moment.

Well, ever since that night, I've been on a roller coaster of emotions and no, I still haven't forgiven. How do I know that? I still want that person to hurt, I still want revenge; see…right there, I haven't forgiven. Forgiveness does not want to retaliate, or harm or wish harm to another person in any way. It's letting go of all the thoughts of bitterness and resentment. Now deep down, I really don't want to be the source of hurt for another person, but maybe someone else could inflict them instead. Human nature can cause us to be very immature at times when there is a deep pain, I'm sorry to say I was guilty of that. It reduces a person to one that is not very desirable. I became the person I disliked because of my behavior and thoughts. How did I get here? I was grown up, reasonable, and oh so mature! Well, what I discovered is that I am not immune to all these qualities when deeply hurt.

Where was my intuition in all of this? I was mad at God for a while. Why didn't my intuition warn me? Or did it, but I wasn't listening? Too clouded with emotion, discernment of what was intuition, and what was my emotion eluded me. That dream I had, was it just a bad dream, or in fact, my intuition?

Bad dream, that's what I told myself. My insecurities crept in, so I thought it was something that was bothering me, which I dealt with and carried on. There were other question marks being raised in my mind. I thought I would wait until we talked in person, as texting or phone calls are not the way to communicate for discussions with any emotional depth. I was learning that the hard way as well. Too many misunderstandings coupled with seemingly mixed messages and more confusion on top of uncertainty; that's a recipe for disaster.

I still wonder, what happened? Was there something I did that hurt this person, and therefore I was being repaid? Was this a form of revenge? I still don't know. What I don't understand is how two seemingly mature adults would choose to communicate through immature actions. Had I done that? Well, there was an incident where I should have picked up the phone and explained something, but I texted about my plans for the next week. Looking back, this texting thing just doesn't work for me with real, honest, caring relationships or friendships when trying to make important plans. Did that warrant the betrayal? Another misunderstanding and one that I tried to clarify, but it was too late, the damage had been done. There we were in a gulf of silence, each with our own private thoughts weighing on our minds. To this day, I still have unanswered questions.

It's hard to forgive when you don't know the whole story; at least it is for me. It's easy to rationalize, take the blame, justify and hold on while thinking, maybe this isn't what it seems, or maybe I've got it all wrong. The vicious cycle of doubt and denial spins around in my head, emotions intense and I felt sick again. I knew better, I knew what my intuition was trying to tell me. I just wouldn't listen. Rather, didn't want to listen; simple as that... no mystery there! Had I been...oh, what's the word...courageous, or brave or smart, yes, had I been smart, I would have just asked right then and there, at that moment, was this true? There...that would have ended this whole thing. There is my answer; I wasn't ready for it to be over. Now, it's back to being my fault again, get mad at myself and then forgive myself after crying a flood of tears. Go back to my original conclusion, a line was crossed and I will someday forgive, but reconciling is clearly not in the present or future.
To get to the end of this, is really what I need.

I take a break, walk out to the kitchen and catch the soft, cool breeze that blows though my window. I let it clear the air and my frazzled mind so that I can think again, rationally. Suddenly, lyrics wrapped in a melody come to my mind, pen on paper, voice to recorder, another song being born, my therapy, my release. All I know at this point is I want it to be over and done with. I'm tired of reliving, feeling, digging deep over and over and crying. This messy, painful process is too much; I need relief.

Boundaries established now, intuition revisited and recorded, dream reviewed, my learning has begun, and there is no point beating up myself for this mistake. You see, I had a reason for waiting to clear things up with this person face to face, which I think is valid. The body language, eye contact, not texting or phoning, this is the reality needed to prevent misunderstandings and the hurt that led to betrayal. That time of honesty never came, that opportunity missed. For some, it's easier to act than to deal with truth.

My prayer: God, I ask you to please take all the ugliness I feel from inside of me. Please lift the anger and heal my heart. I'm done. I don't want this heartache anymore, please remove it from me.

I release this person from my angry grip. I forgive this person, I forgive myself. I weep. I weep some more, for a few weeks. In time, I'm moved toward compassion as I no longer want anything but blessings and mercy for this person.

I will probably never speak forgiving words in person. I know I have done all I can do in this forgiveness process. I realize forgiving does not require reconciliation. I urge you, if you are in the midst of forgiving, remember that all the negative affects a person throughout the whole body, mind, soul, and spirit. Keep with the process! It's important for your health and your freedom. I have learned that as long as I am honest, asking God to help me forgive others and myself, and to heal me, He will. Forgiveness is a beautiful gift! I like this peace I feel now. My heart feels lighter, my eyes are brighter and I am free! All is well with my soul! Thank you God!!

Donna Davis

Donna Davis is a modern day Mary Poppins with over 30 years of child care/education experience, teaching children through play and laughter. As a lifelong resident of New Jersey, she enjoys nature, food, and adventure. On any given day you can find her sharing smiles as well as a little mischief. ☺

Donna is the founder of, 'The Global Forgiveness Project', a global forgiveness movement. Please join in and connect with others to celebrate how forgiveness has improved your life and the lives of those around you. She invites you to participate and make a difference in your own life today!

You can reach Donna at:

Email: dynamicddavis@gmail.com

Website: www.TheGlobalForgivenessProject.com

Website: www.TheMenopauseFairy.com

Phone: (973) 746-1376 (Accepts messages from around the world)

Mailing Address: 41 Watchung Plaza Suite 502, Montclair, New Jersey 07042

The Missing Peace
By Donna Davis

There are times in our life when we realize we have carried pain in our mind, body, soul, and spirit for far too long. These thoughts and feelings have troubled us, stopped us, paralyzed us, and prevented us from living fully, lovingly, and abundantly. The load has been cumbersome and agonizing. We tend to relive these events over and over in our mind to no true benefit. Our perceptions of life, ourselves, and others have become jaded and clouded by all the hurt. Can you honestly say or feel that these thoughts have helped you? Is there any good that they do at all?

There comes a time to lay them down, let them go, and walk away, for good.

We may feel empty of love and support, yet be full of bitterness and resentment at the same time. There is something missing in our lives: PEACE.

Of course, we feel justified for feeling this way. After all it's because SOMEONE ELSE said/didn't say something, or did/didn't do something. How can it have anything to do with us? It's always someone else's fault and come hell or high water THEY are going to pay for all the torment!!! The strange thing is the event or conversation has long been over with and WE are the ones feeling miserable. WE are the ones paying for it. Why do we allow ourselves to be punished for the actions and words of others? Why do we have to feel so offended and put-off by other people and their points of view that may have nothing to do with us at all? The comments or actions from another are their own ideas and perceptions of life. We have our own, a lot of times they don't match up and they don't have to.

AS A CHILD – Who is steering the ship?

I struggled with being the child of two alcoholics. I was hurt, angry, rejected, neglected, lonely, and scared. Being a parentified child at an early age left me feeling helpless and hopeless. I carried this attitude well into my forties. It did not serve me well and people felt sorry for me. It was consoling and gave me the attention I craved. It did little to help me grow; it helped to strengthen the wounds and kept me spinning within them. Even though school was a safe haven for me, I struggled with trust and self-worth. I did make a few friends along the way, but was disappointed in teachers, students, and family who didn't or couldn't help me; Life was difficult. Lessons on all levels needed to be learned.

We tend to think parents can and will fulfil all of our needs and wants. Often we may find that's not the case. We get extremely dejected and hurt, sometimes even crushed. We compare our life to the seeming lives of others and feel short-changed. We frequently feel worse and the saga continues.

Yes, parents are responsible for the safety and welfare of their children. Since children, planned or otherwise, don't come with instruction manuals and grandparents may not be great role models, parents can get easily overwhelmed and not do all that they are supposed to. Our parents may have their own pain and suffering, as you may later find out, that has passed unto them and us through conscious or unconscious means. They did the best they could even though you may have needed more, even though it may not have been enough for you. People cannot give you what they do not have, no matter how badly you need them to.

WITH A PARTNER - The I DO's cant' fix the THEY DIDN'Ts

Still so angry and hurt I went to college to run away from home. There is where I met and married my abusive husband. Misery loves company! Being skilled at saying the right thing at the right time, he lured me with attention and gifts that seemed to fill the void of loneliness that I knew all too well; I just wanted to be loved. I expected him to pick up all the slack and fill all the spaces that my childhood left empty. This set me up for doom and gloom, little did I know that I was the prey and the hunter was merciless and cunning.

We sometimes feel our partners can help or even rescue us from our suffering. Even if they are healthy to do so, that is not their responsibility. They are humans too trying their best to make their lives better alongside you, not because of you. You may be supportive and encouraging, but you can never save one another. You can be beside each other with love and kindness while each person works out their own situations. Your compassion and strength can help guide them to find their own. If the partner is broken, depending on your partner can take a heavy toll on you and the marriage, making things worse.

TAKING A LOOK AT OURSELVES – A shattered mirror

I often blamed myself for not knowing better for allowing these things to happen, and very angry that people took advantage of me. I thought that if I could just understand or justify the mistreatment somehow it would make sense and not happen anymore. I was so willing to have it be my fault, just to have someone to be accountable for all the agony. I thought about it so hard and often that I actually started to believe that I somehow deserved all the abuse.

I became angrier and bitter, always questioning and wondering, "Why me?" I was angry at myself, my parents, God, the world, everything and everyone, without exceptions. I thought if I could just control the situations, the outcomes would be different, better, and less painful. This obsession consumed me and I became a miserable perfectionist in an out of control environment. The anger turned to misery, misery to bitterness, the bitterness into rage, and then into fury. There seemed to be no escaping it.

I finally realized that everything was not my fault or responsibility; I could barely control myself, let alone other people, that was their job. They were their own responsibility. Not an easy transition, but one worth seeing through. I was learning that we all make mistakes and they are a part of life. Somehow, somewhere I may have hurt other people unintentionally while trying to survive and I didn't want to continue down this road of regret and heartache. How do you learn to heal? Where do you start? Who can help? It was time to start living consciously. I had to find out how to do that.

I didn't want to manage my anger and anguish, I wanted to resolve it. I was willing to take full responsibility for myself; my actions, words, thoughts, and decisions. At first our feelings do need to be sorted and managed just to see the big picture and what we are really dealing with. No matter how scary, these thorns must be looked at and looked into to dissolve their charge and make ourselves whole again. It's time to heal.

We owe it to OURSELVES to forgive others. To let ourselves out of the bondage and cages of confinement that imprison us and set ourselves free to live life to the fullest. To find our missing PEACE is the greatest gift we can give to ourselves.

Those who have harmed us, intentionally or not, are not let off the hook with without accountability. What they did, (or didn't do) is indisputable. We DESERVE to live happy, full lives that are not governed by anger and resentment. No matter the reason or cause.

A wise man once spoke to me about my unforgiveness. He said, "It's like drinking poison and expecting the <u>other</u> person to die!" That was shocking. It made me think. It helped me decide. Did I want to continue to feel this way or did I want a chance at a better life, a happier one, a healthier one?

We have a choice. Stay grounded in the fear and agony that has built up over time, or decide to be there for ourselves despite the fact that others' have hurt us and could not/did not give us what we so desperately needed. Although it is not easy or quick I decided to stand up, let go, and LIVE as a testament to MYSELF, that *I* am and always will be there for ME even if no one else is!

Won't you join me? You don't have to do it alone. You don't have to do it at all, but I do know that you will be glad once you do. Be brave, lean on others who have already experienced this shift. Is today the day that your sentence is over?

Please visit (www.TheGlobalForgivenessProject.com) and join me and many others who have experiences with forgiveness and those who are ready to do so now.

Ellie Isacs

Ellie Isacs is a Woman, mamma, Mind and Life Trendsetter Coach, Author, Speaker, a Rebel in Style, and a girl with her own trend. Ellie is the founder of, 'VIDESIGN', and the brain behind the breakthrough coaching system, "Let's Get SELF-ish". She coaches highly successful women, who feel unfulfilled and missing out on life, to find love, happiness, inner fulfilment, and a life on their own terms.

Her mission: "Re-birthing people's SELF and ending the epidemic of, "I am not good enough."

Ellie is passionate about guiding people to get unstuck, move through heartbreak and pain, and thrive on the other side.

You can reach Ellie at:

Website: www.videsign.com

Faccbook: www.facebook.com/elijanaisacs

Pinterest: www.pinterest.com/EllieIsacs

Email: info@videsign.com

From An Empty Womb to a Life Revealed

By Ellie Isacs

This chapter is not about my story. It is about you forgiving yourself.

Let's begin...

"I will never abort a child!" This was my declaration when I was little and I thought nothing in the world would ever make me change my mind.

26 years later

"I love you, but I am not in love with you." Those were the words I heard from the man whom I was supposed to marry. So it began. I knew he was the one and time wouldn't stop me from making him fall in love with me again.

My mission to deserve his love and have him cherish me again took over my entire life. He wanted to be with me, but needed to feel, "in love," again. My attachment to him and the need to be loved was so deep, that nothing stopped me from fulfilling every wish, demand or condition he came up with. I was woven into a web of lies, betrayal, and the belief that it was my fault he wasn't in love with me anymore. If only I had been treating him better, if only I had done as he asked!

Growing up thinking that happiness comes from pleasing people, it wasn't difficult for me to fall deep into the hole of self-deprivation, remorse, and guilt. I invented methods and tools of making him happy, unheard of and nowhere to be found. I read books, watched movies, and spoke to relationship counsellors. I spent money, time, efforts, and energy on becoming the perfect one for him. I became so inventive and giving; I lost track of anything else that was going on with my life. HE had to want me again!

He, on the other hand, turned out to be a very toxic man. The kind of man that sucks you dry over a long period of time until you wake up one day having lost your life and mind. The one that has you pleasing him at all cost. The kind that kills your self-esteem, pride, opinion, needs, personality, and keeps you around hooked. He spoke of love, but could never love. He was the kind of man that will abuse you daily, while manipulating your mind and heart.

One sunny day, walking down the street, I passed by a pharmacy. Something made me stop and think, "How late are you with your period?" Late. I quickly got a pregnancy test and went home to check it out.

Pregnant!

My body froze, my heart sank, I dropped down crying, and all I could hear was, "I love you, but I am not in love with you".

I picked up the phone in my enormous pain and called him…The answer was:

"If you love me, you will abort. I do not want a child now and this will really prove to me you love me and we can be together and build a life."

I don't think there are words that can describe the feeling of having to choose between the man you love leaving you or aborting your child and staying with him. I spent the next three months trying to make a decision. He was unmovable; if you keep the baby, I am gone.

On several occasions I asked him to leave, just so I could have the chance to make a decision without him, one way or another, he didn't. It was a sick game, pretending there was love and care, but actually just an attempt to win at all cost.

I had no support system or family around. My mind was battling between the rationale and the emotions, sounding something like, "It is not possible. I have responsibilities to my other son already, who is paying the price of my divorce. A baby, potentially without a father, with no help, no security, no job. NO vs FUCK IT, I will find a way. I am blessed with a child!!!!"

Having him around gave me the subconscious feeling that he would not go at the end. I went to psychiatrists, therapists, associations to help me make a decision. It was a long, heart-breaking journey. I developed panic attacks, sending me in to the ER constantly.

It was three long months of darkness, desperation, fear, pain, lies, betrayal, manipulation, hospitals, and one almost dead woman – me.

16 weeks into my pregnancy, I had my abortion. I was laying in the operating room, staring at the ceiling in something that resembled a painting. The paradox of looking at art exactly in that moment!

He was in the room. I reached for his hand and whispered, "Can we keep her, please?" He looked at me and without a single emotion showing on his face or a spoken word, he left the room. Tears streaming down my face, I dove into the haze of numbness and the deepest pain I had ever experienced in my heart.

That day I decided that I was going to make this my path and not fall into the conditioning from outside. I decided that I will grieve, but not be a victim of my past.

The next day I collected all the clothes I had bought (my body was starting to change already) and went to return them. I took her picture, vitamins, books, pamphlets, and booklets – everything that had anything to do with this pregnancy and threw them out. I decided that she and I had a bond, which didn't need pictures or books.

During my pregnancy, I searched for answers and help online. I was looking for the support a woman needs when she is facing one of the most difficult decisions in life. I was sickened by the vast amount of negativity around the topic. The enormous guilt provoking articles, pain inflicting propaganda, and efforts to stop you from aborting at all cost. All I was looking for was a place of real support in my decision process. All I found was judgment, stigma, and unrealistic expectations of women. All I could read or hear was, "If you abort, you are a monster. You are killing a child. You are stopping a heartbeat. You will never be the same. This will haunt you to your grave"

If you are reading those lines and are faced with this decision yourself, please hear this from me, "Your situation is unique and nobody can tell you what is best for you. Know that you are important. Know that you are strong. Know that there will be difficulties whatever choice you make, but you have to make sure that the cost you pay either way does not end up being detrimental to you. Abortion is not a choice; it is a responsibility a woman chooses to take! The judgment from outside will not matter if you keep away from judging yourself. You are allowed to make a decision, which is congruent and true for you. If you are alone, know that people can give you tons of advice, but it is you who has to go through it – losing a baby or raising one. YOU MATTER and YOU HAVE A CHOICE how to live your life"

During the days following my abortion, I allowed myself to look at children, babies, toddlers, and smile at them. I learned from the internet that I will never be able to look at children and if I do I will cry. I learned from my experience that I will always look at children and when I do, I smile. I am not a monster.

I invested in energetic healing and release. I allowed myself to mourn, feel, laugh, and cry. I did not judge myself for feeling joy at moments. I didn't force myself and there were moments, in which I was not 100% focused on the loss – and that was ok.

Then I decided to FORGIVE myself for everything; for trusting him, loving him, the abortion, the pain, and for my choices and decisions. I made the choice to walk into the world again and not feel the guilt and remorse for the rest of my life.

We are quick to forgive others, but when we choose to forgive ourselves we get stuck. We are not taught that we deserve love and forgiveness.

Forgiving myself gave me the unique chance to really start over and learn from my experience, instead of having it haunt me like a dark cloud through my entire life.

Forgiving myself didn't mean the abortion did not happen. On the contrary, it meant it did happen and I grew from it. It was a process of sitting with my emotions and feeling them. It was a journey of recognizing that I made a decision based upon what I knew and had in that particular moment. It was a path that allowed me to love her and myself. It was the light, which led me to my freedom.

The freedom you deserve, as well.

I let her go, so I can live and for that, I forgive myself.

Freyja P. Jensen

Freyja is an energetic, effervescent, polished Human Resources Recruitment and Networking Professional. She is a Relationship Manager and Business Consultant, Social Entrepreneur, and the Executive Ninja. She is a Mother, Grandmother, Sister, Daughter, and valued friend. Freyja is a Make-up Artist, Model, published Writer, and an International Best-selling Author for her contribution to the, 'Inch by Inch Growing in Life', book collaboration. Freyja is a Practitioner of Life, game-changer, risk-taker, world-traveller, and fluent in several languages. She has jumped out of planes, and danced in 24 hour dance marathons for charity. She loves to sing and deliver poetry readings, and next on her list is white water rafting!

Having overcome a life-time of adversity, pain, abuse, loss, and bullying, she chose forgiveness in order to move beyond the pain, and that has strengthened her resolve to embrace my passion for life and people with empathy and grace.

As a Practitioner of Life, her legacy and wish, is to create hope, courage, and self-love in others, to realize their own value, to teach them how to become stronger and free of their burdens and to live full, happy, healthy, and loving lives through sustainable change.

As a champion for change, being brave and being victorious in her own personal growth, has allowed her to be a fierce advocate for those who have yet to find their voice by using her own through her writing and public speaking engagements and volunteerism. She is involved with an organization that is very dear to her heart delivering an on-going campaign that is making immense strides and which she believes will have significant impact in making the world a better place by being a part of it. www.openforchange.com

"Leaving a legacy of LOVE is about putting love into action and sustaining it for a better world by making the world a better place to live in." ~Freyja P. Jensen #IAMOFC

My Saving Grace – Mastering Unconditional Forgiveness

By Freyja P. Jensen

How do I possibly share the extent of what my heart has learned about Forgiveness in 1500 words or less? In my last chapter that I shared in the International Best Selling book collaboration, "Inch by Inch Growing in Life" I talked about overcoming adversity as a child. Here I will speak of **Grace found through Forgiveness.**

When she came to our home, I felt rescued. Finally someone to love, see, hear, care for us since my birth Mother was killed in front of my eyes in a horrific train crash when I was seven that traumatized me. When Dad decided to marry again, it was to a woman whom he knew and was to marry before meeting my birth Mother.

She was a care-giver but also an abuser without even realizing the effects of her actions. It wasn't until I visited with my son when he was three years old and asked her why she never held him, showed affection to him, loved him as the adorable, sweet grand-child that he was, that I realized that she was incapable of truly loving unconditionally. She said, how could she love him when he wasn't her own flesh & blood, that if it was the child of her own son, she would feel differently. That revelation turned my guts inside out and I remember being nauseated by the effect of her words piercing my heart. So my retort was, "That means you never loved us like your own either" and her response, "How could I, you are not my children."

Torment, torture, taunting, bullying through slander, verbal, physical and psychological abuse, telling me that I was ugly and a whore like my Mother and that I deserved to be punished. She sat idly by while my Father punished and shamed me in front of my brothers, allowing the horrific punishments to occur while she stood by as a witness, a collaborator, as a woman, let alone a Mother. One would have a hard time fathoming her character being one of love.

After the visit with my son, I swore to never step foot into their home again.

Nearly 12 years later the most revealing moment of awakening occurred during a Christian Easter weekend retreat. It awakened me to a life-changing experience. It was then that I realized if someone far greater than me could love me so unconditionally, forgive my every transgression, and love me undeniably and whole-heartedly without question, that I had the capacity to do the same. If we are created in the image of our heavenly Father, and in the biblical words, cast no stones because we are each guilty of sin and worthy of forgiveness, than I am also capable of the same. It was the catalyst that changed my heart and became the footsteps to my healing, **my saving grace**.

That Easter Sunday evening, I called my Father. After so many years I felt a deep need to make peace. It was time to go home. I remember being on the plane praying fiercely to God to please erase all the pain from the past to allow for hope, peace, love and for me, most importantly, to allow **Forgiveness**, to infiltrate my heart, to show me grace and for a fresh start. The reunion at the airport was filled with happy tears.

I realized after spending some time with my step-Mother, that she was not herself, in fact she was appearing to be a shell of the woman I knew. She was phenomenal with numbers, banking, an excellent housekeeper to the point of fanatical, a great cook and care-giver. There was one crucial flaw in her make-up. Her heart was damaged. So through my own experience of being graced with love, acceptance and forgiveness, it was time for me to extend myself further to showing love to someone that perhaps had never felt loved or loveable. Through all the damage that had taken place, there was one greater tragedy which I had to consider that had affected my sanity and will to live many times over.

When she had arrived and accepted my Father's invitation to marry and stay in Canada, she also brought her child, a son 5 years older than me. When my Dad and step-Mom left for a trip to Germany when I was 12, they left my step-brother in charge of my younger and older brother and me.

One night shortly after our parents left he locked both my brothers into the closet of a bedroom telling them to pretend that they were camping. He proceeded to blind fold and gag me, tie me up, then brutally rape me. Our parents discovered what had happened by finding the bloody sheets and clothes that were hidden away by my step-brother, the rapist. To my Father's credit, he banned him from the house for what he had done. My step-Mother however, was devastated. It was her flesh and blood that was being banished and it was my fault. The punishments never ceased and the abuse I experienced from her never stopped. I would always pay the price for her pain and anger, for her heart-ache and for her past, for both myself and my own Mother.

The visit home then after so many years carried a lot of weight. Seeing her again and realizing she was not well, gave me the opportunity to reflect on the gifts I had been given through my experience at that memorable, life-rendering Easter weekend. I had changed. My heart had changed. I was different. I had the capacity to forgive and the capability to love beyond the pain I had suffered. We were given the diagnosis that my step-Mother was quickly progressing from dementia to Alzheimer's and needed constant care and supervision. Through the next few years I made several visits home to help Dad care for her. She no longer could talk logically nor feed, clothe or bathe herself. I sat with her and read from the Bible. I prayed for her and to her. I sang to her. And although nothing she said made any sense at this point and her thinking was completely scrambled, there were a few moments of clarity. While I sat there next to her, stroking her arm, she turned to me and said, "I was there for you and now you are here for me." I felt the truth in her words. She had been there, good and bad, I learned from this.

That evening while I was in the bathroom cleaning, bathing and diapering her, I looked deep into her eyes and said, "For all the horrible things you did and said to me, I forgive you and for all the mean things I did and said to you, please forgive me." And we both began to weep and sob heart-wrenchingly and I knew to the core of my being that she understood. We made peace that night and there by the grace of God go I. Forgiveness changes people.

She passed away shortly after that. As for my step-Brother, he is somewhere out there. He never came when she passed on while I sat with my Father. He did however call and harass my Father and threaten my son and me for selfish reasons motivated by material things. Wherever he is today, he is paying his own price. I went to see my step-brother prior to my step-Mother's death in hopes of making peace with him and myself. He apologized for what he had done asking for forgiveness and I told him I had done so many years before on that amazing Easter weekend but that it was up to him to forgive himself. I have no idea where he lives now or if he is even alive. He had mentioned once to me that people didn't change but on the contrary, I know for a fact to the core of my being, that people can and do change. Hearts change through grace and forgiveness. My life has changed and I am a better person because of the lessons I have learned.

As an adult I've been diagnosed with PTSD, Anxiety, Depression, Panic, Adrenal Fatigue, IBS and a plethora of digestive issues but in spite of all of that, I remain a VICTOR and not a victim. I lead a positive, productive life. I am an advocate for those who are having difficulties finding their voices. My desire is to leave a legacy of love which is what "Open For Change" means to me; "putting love into action and sustaining it for a better world by making the world a better place to live in." I have good and bad days, but one thing remains strong and steadfast, my passion for life, love, family, friends; people and my undeniable will to live authentically and with purpose.

I am Open For Change, are you? #IAmOFC

www.OpenForChange.com

Rainbow Heart Love & Peace

Glenis Sheeler

Glenis currently lives in Airdrie, Alberta with her 12 year old granddaughter and 14-year-old grandson. She completed her University education in 2002 in Social Work, but has been working in the field for over 20 years. Glenis spent her career working in the crisis field and her strengths are brought to life there. She became a widow very suddenly in June of 2014 and has been emotionally fighting her way back to joy. She is passionate about meeting people and learning their stories and considers counselling a privilege.

You can reach Glenis at:

Email: sheelerglenis@hotmail.com

Ashes to Ashes We All Fell Down
By Glenis Sheeler

Forgiveness? For real? If people only knew what I had done they would wish they had never met me. At least that is what I believed for years, so many years, twenty-two years this month to be exact. I finally started to forgive myself about four years ago and I think I'm finally there!

In 1994, I was a 30 year old mother of three children ages thirteen, twelve, and ten. My husband, their father, was a workaholic and seldom home with us. My eldest daughter was struggling with something and I just couldn't get her to tell me what it was. I tried everything I knew and some things that were suggested by others, but I couldn't connect with her. She was angry all the time and was becoming increasingly mean and angry toward her brother and sister. She seemed to actually hate me more. The harder I tried, the worse it got. I decided to talk to a professional, so I made an appointment with a child psychologist for my daughter and myself as a place to start. I believed if she wouldn't talk to me maybe she would talk to him. I was hopeful and at my wits end. She refused to go! Oh my God, now what? I went anyway. I thought I could possibly learn some skills on how to help her.

I sat with Dr. Neuman and explained how my daughter was behaving and the things I had tried. I described how she continually threatened to run away and the fact that I was at a loss on how best to respond. I couldn't admit that in some of my more stressful moments I actually wished she would! The doctor advised me to call her bluff. He stated she was threatening so often because she was trying to emotionally control the house and it was working. It made sense to me. It was logic that I could wrap my head around. I had a tool from a professional that I could try! I was hopeful again so off I went home to deal with her after school attitude.

Kyla didn't disappoint! She was bitter, sarcastic, and delivered her bullying mentality towards her siblings and me. I was still feeling hopeful from my appointment and I deep breathed my way through. The next morning while Kyla was putting on her shoes for school she was looking at her shoe when she asked THE question. "Mom, what would you do if I didn't come home from school ever again?" I took my deep calming breath and gave my scripted response, "Kyla you need to do what you believe is right. I would miss you, but I would understand." There, I did it! I said it word for word the way the Psychologist said. I was certain there would be a big break through on the way very soon. Kyla never even looked at me or said goodbye when I told her to have a good day. Oh believe me that was normal! It was to be my last 'normal' event with my daughter.

Kyla never came home that day. I drove around throughout the night looking everywhere I could think of. The fear was indescribable. I wasn't sure if I should sit home by the phone or be out searching for her. There were no cell phones then. The next day, I went to the police to report her missing. I intentionally didn't share with them that she may have simply run away because I knew they wouldn't help me. They didn't help anyway because they said based on her age it was most likely she had run away and would return once she realized it wasn't so easy without her family. I knew they were wrong. I don't know how I knew, but I did. They wouldn't take me serious so I was on my own. I had two younger kids and a husband that simply went to work. I drove, searched, and then searched and drove some more. I went to her school and searched through her locker for clues, nothing. I was living in the worst hell I could imagine. My words to her kept running through my mind, "I would miss you, but I would understand." I didn't understand! I was so scared, I couldn't breathe.

Five days. Kyla was missing for five days. A knock at the door came. I opened it and there was my sister and my daughter standing there. She was home! I wanted to hug her and slap her all in the same second! The events began to unfold and I could never have imagined what I heard. Kyla had been picked up at school that Friday afternoon and taken to a small town 40 minutes north of where we lived. Her and her kidnapper spent the first night there then went on the move again, anther two hours north. My heart sunk. I had checked the exact place she had spent her first night, but missed them by no more than an hour. They then rented a hotel room in a town two and a half hours from home and remained there until Kyla got a chance to phone her Auntie to come and get her. Kyla believed she was going to be getting away from a family that made her life awful and that the man taking her was going to make all her thirteen-year-old dreams come true. He ended up abusing her mentally and sexually in ways that I'm certain I'm still unaware of. The kick in the gut was that he was a 73-year-old man. Even worse was that he was the husband of my mother's best friend. It was too much. I couldn't process it all. I tried to, but couldn't.

The next day was spent in a haze that I struggle to recall even now. However, the day after that, I learned that he had discovered people were aware he had taken Kyla, but he did not yet know she was at home. His wife called me and said he had left the house with his rifle and stated he was going to where my daughter was and he was going to kill her and then himself. SHE PHONED ME NOT THE POLICE!! I got off the phone and called the police. The Corporal I spoke with was dismissive and disrespectful. I described how scared we were and he decided he should tell me I didn't know what fear was! It was terrifying knowing he was intent on killing my child! How could we keep her safe??

There was no sleep had that night. The next day we learned he had committed suicide by tying a rope around his neck and the other end around his steering wheel. He got to a speed of 100 MPH on the country road next to ours and jumped out. It was such a brutal death that the news people were all over it. At first it was a suspected murder. His family was devastated and the sympathy was pouring in for them. My family was devastated and so broken. My daughter was guilt ridden because she had wished him dead and blamed herself for it.

I worked hard to let her know it wasn't her fault. She needed to forgive herself. I wanted him alive so I could kill him. However, I did learn to forgive him because it was the only chance of any peace in my heart. After all, he was dead. So, I forgave him and I forgave my daughter. Yet, someone had to be at fault. It was me who told her to do it. It was me who wished she would run away in those moments of extreme frustration. During the times when I would allow myself to forget it was my fault, Kyla would remind me. She allowed me in her life until I made a mistake. Then I was banished again. She has two children. Abby is 11 and Jordan is 13. I am forbidden to see them. She claimed I put my grandson in danger and didn't protect him. It was untrue, but she believes it's in her best interest to remind me to never forget what I did! I made the decision to stop allowing her to blame me, but first, I needed to forgive myself. I believe I did all that I knew how to do. I looked for help from professionals when I needed it and I tried so hard to do the right thing. I believe when you know more you do more. She was held against her will for five days and continues to stay stuck. She and I held me responsible for 18 years. I'm a good person. My sentence has been served, twice over.

Dr. Heidi Westra Brocke

Dr. Heidi Westra Brocke is an 18 year practitioner who has dedicated her career to the health and wellness of others. She is sole owner of Edge Chiropractic & Wellness, where her passion is making people not only feel better, but also feel better about themselves. She, through example, emphasizes to her patients the importance of caring for THEMSELVES not only physically, but also emotionally. She strives to instill the confidence needed to achieve their goals both in health and in life, by encouraging a positive outlook and conveying HOPE.

Dr. Heidi is a proud wife and loving mother. Her belief is that life is about the small things that happen day to day and she is grateful for all the situations her life has led her through. She is able to use life experience to reach her patients at a personal level. Her hobbies include co-owning a boutique, weightlifting and figure competing, decorating her home, time with friends, making people smile, and cowboy boots.

All who have entered her life have led her to the person she is today.

You can reach Dr. Heidi at:

Email: contact@edgewellness.net

Website: www.edgewellness.net

Facebook: www.facebook.com/edgewellnessboutique

Facebook: www.facebook.com/edgechiropracticandwellness

Worth the Wait

By Dr. Heidi Westra Brocke

Forgiveness. Forgiveness is not for the person who has wronged you. Forgiveness is for the person who has been wronged, in order for them to move on to be who they were meant to be without bitterness or scars holding them back.

The small farming community in Montana was the perfect environment to raise children. My strong loving family, a small Christian school, and a supportive community provided me with a sheltered upbringing far from the exposure of the real world. A calm safe place that I assumed would be found everywhere. It was with that perspective at 21 years of age I left to begin my own life. I was a happy confident girl who believed in herself and believed that people were basically good at heart because I had not seen anything to the contrary. I was very trusting and happy to help those in need.

I moved many miles away to begin my career in healthcare. I was excited in anticipation with what life would bring and ready to change the world. The day I met him I had no way of knowing that my happy world would soon slip away to a cold prison like existence.

Years passed and from the outside looking in our marriage appeared loving, the business we shared profitable, and our children adventurous and happy. From the inside looking out it was strikingly not the same. Many years of my life were shared with an obsessively controlling man who was seldom satisfied with the very best I could offer. The longer the relationship went on the more difficult it became for me to ever imagine getting out.

We shared a very successful practice, a small farm, and two beautiful daughters whose talents landed us in the spotlight much of the time. Smiling became an act as I struggled to make it through the endless lies, the devastating put downs, and the insignificance of my wants. I became numb to my own emotions and to his raging outbursts. I accepted this monotony as my life, working every day FOR him, but never as a partner with him in life, business, or parenting.

This positive girl who once laughed now cried and walked with her head down. I lived everyday knowing my opinion didn't matter, my feelings were insignificant, and no matter how hard I tried I would fall just short of approval.

I stayed too long; I stayed out of obligation, out of guilt. I stayed for my kids, my practice, my patients, for all my hard work, and for all the time and money I had invested. Most of all, I had become so fearful of him that I was unable to take the first step to change anything about the situation.

Years passed, my children grew, and I remained frozen in this secluded life. There was even a significant event that led me to file and finalize divorce, but still my fear of him kept me trapped to do his work and pay for his frivolous lifestyle all the while losing more of myself and my children. I was giving up.

Over the long years there were several people who cared about me and offered their assistance, but being paralyzed in what had become normal, I was unable accept their help. Then one day my life changed. My path crossed with a beautiful, calming, stable man who through reasons I cannot explain gave me the courage to take the step I had been unable to take in almost 13 years. Jeremy changed my perspective and believed in me. Through words of encouragement he presented the possibility of hope and peace in my future. Something in this man gave me the reassurance, which extended far above my fears, that all in my life would someday be ok.

The years had dragged on and even after being divorced and in my own home, the control was relentless. I see now though that everything happened just as it was supposed to because by the time Jeremy did enter my life all of the barriers, aside from fear, had been broken. It was perfect timing and it was at that moment I felt free for the first time.

One short week after meeting Jeremy, I walked away from life as I knew it, from a thriving business, a growing practice, my patients of 10 years, away from my friends, away from all I had worked for, and most sadly away from my children. Although I had joint custody of my girls since the divorce, my former, being above the law, kept them from me no matter the expense. I would exhaust myself trying to accommodate him just so I could see my girls.

Now, being raised in a dairy farm with a meagre childhood, I could handle being a business woman without a business, I could handle being a doctor without patients, I did not need a lot of things or money to survive. However, a mother without her children was a harder thing to accept. What kind of mother does that? As heart-breaking as this was, I knew I would have to get out, get stable, and then begin the journey to get my children back. I had left him many times in the past, but not being strong enough to live without my children I always went back. My former ruined my reputation to make him look good, kept my girls from me, and I left this shattered perception of life to start over.

This is where my story begins...

I mentioned before that Jeremy gave me the encouragement to take the first step, which is exactly what it was, THE FIRST STEP.

The years following were filled with many other steps that had to be done entirely by myself. There were steps to rebuild my non-existent confidence, to overcome my programmed way of thinking, and to trusting again. I needed to accept my new role as a distant parent and learn to guide and reassure my girls from afar. I had to learn to put my faith in the fact that my girls would be safe until I could once again be in their lives. I started a new practice and had to go through the steps of growing a new business and to make something out of nothing. Most of all, I had to embrace what it felt like to genuinely love and to be loved without strings and accusations. These steps were an upward battle posing many stalls and setbacks. Eventually though, the often heard harsh words, "you are not good enough, no one will ever respect you, no one will ever love anyone like you," slowly began to fade as they were replaced with, " you are beautiful, you deserve respect, and I want to spend the rest of my life with you." All the hard work and pain was paying off as every day I felt myself get stronger and happier.

Seven years later I am married to the ever loving, patient man who saved me. The road for him was not an easy one either as I struggled to get back to being me. He has never asked me to change a thing about myself; he encourages me in my choices and loves me without conditions.

With words and actions of love for me, I was able to piece my dreams back together. I have taken the opportunity to replace my regrets with lessons learned and have moved only forward.

I am now a successful business woman AGAIN with a growing business, I am a dedicated doctor with many patients, and I am a mother who has been able to develop a strong relationship with my now grown daughters and guide them to respect themselves and use forgiveness in their favor. I am a happy girl again and thankful for the feeling of sunshine on my face. I am grateful for the little things that happen day to day. Most of all I am able to give my love away and give it abundantly to those who are deserving of it.

I spent much of my life asking why I stayed in an unhealthy environment for so long, why I let him beat me down, why I didn't stand up more for myself and my girls, but today I am grateful for each and every circumstance and situation that my life has led me through. With many years of learning I am able to openly help others, feel their pain, and relate to their fears. If I had not walked in the shoes I have; I would not be able to embrace those walking a similar path.

Forgiveness for me does not excuse any of the actions against me, but it has allowed me the freedom to lead, listen, and cry with those yet searching to forgive. I have faith that my experiences in hurt, trial, and pain will continue to be worth the price as I help carry others who are struggling to walk through their own fire.

Jayan E. Romesh

Jayan E. Romesh is an engineer turned author who conveys a simple yet profound message to the world with his timely teachings. He is a two times International Bestselling Author. Jayan has travelled across the world while undergoing an evolutionary transformation himself. Being an engineer by profession, he strives to elevate humanity with technical contributions apart from his writing. He brings his inspiring and loving message to transform the audience giving an opportunity to create a more loving world around us. He lives in Vancouver British Columbia.

You can reach Jayan at:

Facebook: www.facebook.com/jayan.eromesh

Email: jayanromesh@yahoo.com

Website: www.jayanromesh.com

Jayan E. Romesh   CEng (MIET)

The Path to Forgiveness with Loving Kindness

By Jayan E. Romesh

"May I forgive myself for ...,

May I forgive you for ... ,

May you forgive me for ...."

- Meditation on Forgiveness

Seeking happiness has been my life long purpose on this planet. Happiness is our natural state. Cultivation of a mind of unconditional love, forgiveness, and benevolence for all beings constitutes an important part of happiness.

In the past, I searched for the things that I thought would give me material success and happiness. I became habituated by reaching for things that could provide it. I certainly tried many different things and I acquired material items that made me happy and secure. I built relationships that did not have mutual understanding and love. In 2010, affected by war, conflicts, and economic downturn, I was compelled to leave behind my material wealth and travel to Canada in search of safety, peace, and prosperity. My quest did not provide me with the lasting happiness I was looking for as I had to undergo many challenges in a distant land where I lacked love and support.

"Happiness and Peace doesn't exists in a distant land, It lies within us".

- Jayan E. Romesh

In 2012, my life unravelled. In one horrible year, it felt like my life evaporated. I lost everything I acquired in my motherland while away in a distant land searching of peace and prosperity. I was left with nothing, no material reminders of my previous life. Everything was gone and I had to make decisions about how to move on. I thought maybe this was preparing me for some greater lesson that would transform my life. Adversity was preparing me for greatness. I began to realize my life has an outer material purpose and an inner spiritual purpose.

"We must be willing to let go of the life we've planned,

So as to have the life that is waiting for us."

- Joseph Campbell

I was initially filled with grief and hatred towards circumstances and people who I thought created these conditions for me. As my pain began to fade, I gradually let go of the past. I did not react emotionally and instead through the practice of forgiveness I started to break the emotional chains that tied me down. I came to realize,

"By breaking the link that connects feeling and actions, we could create emotional freedom; the key to forgiveness"

I gained personal power through forgiveness and loving kindness to break the habit of feeling like I had no choice. I found that happiness is always a choice and I was then able to tap into the creative potential of my life. I was deeply touched by my inner stillness that gave me the transformation. It had managed to find myself, even in the dark. I started to recognize how precious the human life on this planet is and how we could serve to elevate it and bring some cheerfulness, hope, wellbeing, spiritual growth or ecstasy into the life of another person with a warm heart, compassion, and forgiveness.

"Life is an adventure in forgiveness"

- Norman Cousins

The path to forgiveness is a way of opening up to the possibilities of true healing so that you can send loving kindness to yourself and to others. Forgiveness is a soft gentle way of learning how to lovingly accept whatever arises and to leave it be, without trying to control it with your thoughts. Sit down comfortably with your eyes closed or open. The first step of this practice is to forgive yourself by the following four statements one at a time:

"I forgive myself for not understanding"

"I forgive myself for making mistakes"

"I forgive myself for causing pain to myself or anyone else"

"I forgive myself for not acting the way I should have acted"

Place that feeling of forgiveness in your heart and radiate the feeling through repetition. Initially you will face resistance to forgive yourself, but recognizing, repeating, and staying relaxed, you can return back and start repeating it with a smile.

The next step is to forgive other people for not understanding, making mistakes, for causing pain to themselves and to you, or for not acting in the way they should have acted. Forgive them for everything.

Visualize them in your mind and look into their eyes and forgive them. Keep repeating one of these statements or you can make up your own statement of forgiveness if it seems right.

It is best to forgive them by using the same statement over and over again. "I forgive you for…"

Whenever the mind becomes distracted, softly, gently recognize the distraction and comeback with repeating and relaxing with a smile.

After a period of time, change things around and hear that person forgiving you for… Still look into their eyes and hear them say, "I forgive you too. I really do forgive you".

This forgiveness path starts by forgiving yourself, forgiving another person, and then you hear them forgive you too.

Put forgiveness into everything all of the time. This will develop a loving-acceptance and a true feeling of love toward every situation and every person that caused so much pain. The pain will diminish until there is only a memory of that situation or of that person without any experience of grief. It is necessary to keep this practice going for quite some time so that eventually, upon retraining the mind, you rewire the brain so that all attachments will be let go of automatically.

When my hatred ceased and it became easier to treat others with love and forgiveness, there were no more struggles in my life. I felt spontaneous forgiveness for the people who had done me wrong. Through forgiveness, I have found a balanced from the inside that helps to temper my reactions and I feel a genuine willingness to accept and forgive. I also feel free to express love for all living beings with kindness.

"To understand everything is to forgive everything."

\- Lord Buddha

Although I lost my material wealth, I have found my true wealth that is the radiant joy of being and the deep, unshakable peace that comes with forgiveness. Contentment is the greatest wealth. I look in at a treasure within that is infinitely greater than anything the world could offer me. My negative thoughts lost power over me and I feel a certain stillness and peace inside me. With the practice of forgiveness, the sense of stillness and peace has deepened and feel a subtle emanation of joy arising from deep within, the joy of being. The whole external world has become insignificant to me and I evolved into a selfless state with a connection to all beings.

"By forgiveness you change your future"

I have come to know that challenges are gifts, opportunities to learn. I have learned lessons from my setbacks and made them as opportunities to increase   acceptance, forgiveness, flexibility, patience, compassion, joy, and equanimity. Genuine boundless love and forgiveness for everything makes me feel like life has powerful possibilities. It created happiness from within, a profound sensation with inner stillness that endures the true happiness.

Finally I have learned to allow the present moment to be and to just accept the impermanent nature of all things and conditions with forgiveness for everything. Forgive every thought, every memory. Forgive every pain that arises.

My thoughts will be constructive, never destructive. My mind will dwell in the present moment with forgiveness that has infinite possibilities. It will not dwell in the past, which is a mere illusion. I will seek the association of those who are working and striving to bring about positive changes in the world. I am finding peace and lasting happiness on this planet.

"Forgiveness is the fragrance that the violet sheds

On the heel that has crushed it.

It is the sun rays that light up the clouds that

Has tried to cover it.

Be the light of the world with forgiveness and love"

\- Jayan E. Romesh

"May All Beings Be Safe

May All Beings Be Happy

May All Beings Be Healthy

May All Beings Live with Ease"

- Meditation on Loving Kindness

Jenny Gaudreau-Dumont

Jenny Gaudreau-Dumont helps people *live their happily ever after.* Jenny is an International Best Selling Author, Area Director with BNI, and Founder of 'A Place for Grace Child Care.'

Jenny works with professionals to uncover exactly *why* they do what they do, so they can attract the kind of customers they really can help – all through building strong personal networking groups with BNI. Her passion for helping others achieve success is grounded in her motto, "live your happily ever after."

As Founder of 'A Place for Grace Child Care' Jenny created her daughter's happily ever after by giving her the perfect place to spend non-school time. 'A Place for Grace' is a child care center for special needs children in Saginaw, Michigan. Jenny has taken her passion and her love for her daughter, Emma Grace, and shared it with other families with special needs children. Jenny's journey of forgiveness makes 'A Place for Grace Child Care' even more personal.

You can reach Jenny at:

Website: www.jennydumont.com

Website: www.aplaceforgracechildcare.org

Email: jennyd@aplaceforgracechildcare.com

Facebook: www.facebook.com/jenny.gaudreaudumont.com

My Life Purpose Hidden in a Tragedy, A Path of Self Forgiveness
By Jenny Gaudreau-Dumont

"What is the meaning of life?" "What is my purpose in life?" Many people ponder these the age old questions for their entire life and engage in therapy and self-healing retreats trying to figure it out. When faced with life altering events, the answer to an unanswered question can hit you square in the face.

When my then husband and I made the conscious decision to have a child together, it was an exciting time in our lives. We were newly married, both for the second time, in love and wanting to have something we shared together. How joyful we were to learn of our pregnancy after only trying for a short period of time. That joy and excitement quickly turned to heartbreak and blame.

At 33, I was considered high risk and so when I was told that I was referred to a specialist for a level two ultrasound because something on our daughter's face looked abnormal, I figured they were making something out of nothing, and it was routine. Their reasoning, it appeared she had an abnormally large nose. My husband's facial features were larger, so for her to have a larger appearing nose, I thought nothing of it.

My husband hadn't planned to attend the ultrasound with me, however, his mother was in town and she decided to attend with me at the last minute. The doctor immediately found her cleft lip and palette and proceeded to inform me that a cleft lip and palette were indicators for Trisomy 13, having an extra 13 chromosome. He stated very matter-of-fact that Trisomy 13 babies don't live long past birth and that if I wanted to find out if she had it, I could do an amniocentesis. However, I could choose not to and just find out when she was born. My life changed forever in a matter of 15 minutes! I can still feel every single second of those 15 minutes, even 10 years later. I was in shock. I didn't cry or react. I immediately went to my husband's work and as I proceeded to inform him of the outcome of the appointment, I broke down.

We ultimately made the decision to have the amniocentesis and were very happy to find out she did not have Trisomy 13. She did however, have a heart murmur, a midline bilateral cleft lip and palette, and a two vessel cord. My poor baby girl! I was completely helpless.

We now had 20 more weeks to plan and prepare for her arrival and the post birth plans. We first choose a name, Emma Grace.

I researched all about cleft lips and facial deformities and their causes. We met with surgeons and therapists and doctors and I always asked them the same question, "how did this happen?" Of course, no one could tell me one good answer. So naturally, I blamed myself.

What did I do before I knew I was pregnant that caused her to have these problems? Did I drink when I shouldn't have? Did I expose her to some chemicals I didn't know about? Did I eat something bad, exercise too much, have sex when I shouldn't have, or was I stressed? I racked my brain and couldn't get passed it. The blaming got worse.

I will never forget seeing the pictures from the oral surgeon on what to expect when she was born. It was heart wrenching. To think that my little Emma Grace would have to endure surgeries every 2 to 3 months her first year of life was not something I had prepared for. This was supposed to be a joyous time and all I could do was question myself as a mother and continue the blame game. Nothing I could possibly say to myself made any difference; it had to be my fault.

I really tried to put on a good face to everyone for the remainder of my pregnancy. No one knew what to really say except, "they have come a long way with surgeries for babies, I am sure everything will be ok". What did they know anyway? I was angry and resentful and I continued to blame myself and felt miserable and helpless.

When Emma Grace was born it seemed like everything was so normal, except it wasn't. She was born in respiratory distress and I got to see her for 30 seconds before they took her to NICU. Poor thing had a broken clavicle, which I didn't know about until 9 days later, was jaundice, had a brain infection, and of course, the bilateral cleft lip and palette.

The only thing that got me through the entire day was knowing that I had to be strong for her because she was an innocent little baby and it was my fault she was born this way. There was just no way for me to think any other way. There is a parable in the bible that talks about the man born blind, and how the community of people thought that the parents must have been sinners for their son to be born blind and they weren't worthy of having God's love. As a parent, it is very easy to feel that way when your innocent child has so many medical issues at birth.

Days after Emma's birth, I felt guilty for everything that I had in my own hospital room because she had nothing, and she was suffering. It gave me perspective on life that I had never contemplated before. My view of everything changed. Having a baby was supposed to be one of the most joyous times of your life, expect, how could I be happy when there was so much she was going through? It was entirely my fault!

I have heard of stories of forgiveness that make my heart swell. People forgive others who have committed grave crimes against the ones they love, even murder. People forgive the ones they love for acts of violence, infidelity, lies, and stealing. Stories of people forgiving themselves are far less spoken. Forgiving yourself involves so much more than I could possibly contemplate. No matter how many times people told me that it wasn't my fault, and that it was God's will, I couldn't see it. Why would God put an innocent child through so much?

Today, Emma Grace is one of the most happy, loving, and genuine 10 year old girls I have ever known. Her crooked sweet smile melts my heart and I couldn't imagine her any other way.

Over time, the guilt was less intense because the surgeries were over for a while and we had a plan to deal with her cognitive impairments and her developmental delays. She was making progress. It wasn't until she was suddenly diagnosed with epilepsy that it all came back like a roaring ocean wave! Watching her go through such traumatic and violent seizures was horrifying. It took every prayer I had to keep strong for her. I still didn't see how this could be God's will!

I will never forget the day that God's will was shown to me. As I walked out of daycare on the fourth day in a row of being called to pick her up because of an emotional meltdown, I asked myself why wasn't there a daycare for kids like Emma, where she could just be like every other kid, and the staff know how to take care of her so she didn't have emotional meltdowns? There has to be a daycare for kids with special needs? Well, there wasn't! I was shocked by this revelation and I knew that I had to do something. I may not be able to change Emma's life, but I can certainly change the way she lives in her life!

My heart felt like it was the right thing to do and this was my opportunity to turn my frustration and guilt into something good and embrace the gifts my daughter gives me, as opposed to always thinking about what I took away from her. In reality, she didn't see her life any different than any other child. She was so happy in her life and enjoyed everything! I finally realized that it was only me who was seeing her life as traumatic and felt like she was missing out on what could have been. She wasn't living that way, she was just living her life and it was time I embraced it too and lived it whole heartily with her.

After that day, I set a course to start 'A Place for Grace Child Care'. My vision was to have a daycare specifically for special needs children. It would be a center to serve and honor children with cognitive and emotional impairments, autism spectrum disorder, developmental delays, and speech and language delays. The staff would be trained specifically to manage potential triggers that caused emotional meltdowns and give the kids a place to learn how to develop friendships, engage in social activities and have fun. They would be able to be themselves without feeling they have to conform.

Upon further research, I was astounded to learn that there were over 6,000 children in our county that qualified for special education and that there was no daycare to serve them.

The journey hasn't been easy and there has been many times when I thought I should give up, but my desire to give my Emma Grace a place for her to feel welcomed, loved, and supported for who she is persevered through it all and we opened the doors to 'A Place for Grace Child Care' on September 2, 2014 with 9 kids registered to attend! We now have plans to expand across the state of Michigan.

Some people might say that Emma Grace was given to me, but I believe that I was meant to be Emma Grace's Mother, so I could help her, and many other children just like her, live a full and happy life. What started out as a tragedy in my mind has turned into my life's purpose and without being able to look past the guilt and blame, and forgive myself, I would have never been able to make it happen.

On the other side of forgiveness, you find love and purpose.

Jill Gjorgjievski

Jill Gjorgjievski is a Multi-Dimensional Healer/Teacher| RN |Early Childhood Teacher| Certified Intuitive Life Coach| International Author. She is a Master in Angelic Reiki, Unicorn Healing Energy, Faery Reiki, with the power of Love Energy Healing, and she teaches these modalities.

Jill Gjorgjievski is the founding CEO / Director of Gjorgjievski Enterprises, with the power of Love, Chocolates and Things. Her vision and mission in life is to help people achieve balance and success in life using the highest vibration of love.

You can reach Jill at:

Website: www.jgjorgjievski.com

Website: www.jillgjorgjievski.com

Website: www.withthepoweroflove.com

Facebook: www.facebook/jillgjorgjievski

Skype: Jill.Gjorgjievski

LinkedIn:

www.linkedin.com/au.linkedin.com/pub/jill-gjorgjievski80|82b|929

Google Plus: www.plus.google.com/102253108963879351612/about

Email: jgjorgjievski@yahoo.com.au

Cut and Polished: A Beautiful Facet of You

By Jill Gjorgjievski

When Kate announced her fourth book, I felt a strong urge to be part of this venture. I acknowledged my feelings at the time and knew this was important somehow, but did not act on it immediately. Previously, I had co-authored in two International Best Selling books and I loved the experience of working with other International authors. Weeks went by and the intensity grew every time I saw this title through social media; it kept touching something within me to take action. During that time, I was also working on my own book and had signed up to co-author another book. Hence, I was a little hesitant to make a move based on my intuition, but when I finally took action and I saw the sub-title, "Overcoming the Impossible". I instantly knew I was on the right path. This was how I felt about my last few years, and I thought to myself, "That's my story!"

My journey has been one of forgiveness of myself and others, to overcome what I thought, 'was impossible.' When my late husband made his sudden transition to the spirit world in 2011, his departure had an impact on me in many different ways. I experienced feelings of guilt because I was unable to help him even though I am a nurse and run an Angelic Reiki healing practice. Then, the night of the funeral, I had a stroke. I was unable to visit the grave as our religious practice demanded, and I felt guilty about that as well. There were other factors creating stress. My late husband and I were caring for his father who had dementia. Now I had to handle that on my own. Due to my stroke,

I had no other option, but to put my father-in-law into care, creating more guilt and backlash from extended family and community.

There was also a loss of income when my husband departed, creating greater pressure for me. When I had the stroke, I was unable to work in my chocolate business, which had been growing rapidly and had reached a massive growth milestone by its third birthday. Although my daughter stepped in to take over, my customers did not come in as much because they thought that I was about to close the business due to my circumstances and they wanted me to be there. This had a financial impact on my business income. The banks also created more stress for me as they did not implement a period of mourning for repayments on a joint loan we had for other investments. They demanded full payment of the loan and as I was unable to do this, they took court action and that humiliated and shattered me, as I had made sure I had a squeaky-clean credit rating and did everything by the book only to have it all crumble around me in a split of a second. This caused a self-doubt and distrust in many people. If that was not enough, others took to social media and tried to shame me into compliance to their deadlines. It seemed impossible for one person to deal with all of this and be okay. I was afraid, angry, anxious, and every other emotion one can feel. I thought I could not do it, I felt that it was all too much for one person to handle. As I became more and more overwhelmed by the problems, I experienced lack of self-confidence and at one point defeated. No one believed I could do it and most importantly of all I did not believe in me. Many times, I would sit and think, "Why me?" One day I said to myself, "Why not you Jill? You are capable, otherwise you would not have this challenge." Before anything could change in my outer world, I had to work on myself and overcome these issues. As I took the time and made decisions that were beneficial to me and not according to other people's schedules or deadlines, I overcame the fear and self-doubt, and let it go, I became successful again. This was all part of my learning process.

Things began to turn around. I healed myself physically, emotionally, spiritually, and financially using Angelic Reiki and I am better than ever. I began to shed the old me, but sometimes as we all do at times, got caught up in old patterns and behaviors. When this happens we start to take our lives, other people, and situations for granted.

Spring brings with it a sense of renewal, and I have found it was the perfect time to re-invent myself. I started S-T-R-E-T-C-H-I-N-G away from traditions, obligations that no longer serve a purpose or that have proven to be harmful, and that hold my spirit back. I began to see clearly; have a new vision of myself, my world, my reality. I had scratched the surface of a knowing that truly, all things are created equal, that we are all one. I familiarized myself with a distant memory, that I am a creator and felt myself wanting to learn more on how to liberate myself further. My Heart Chakra began healing and opening to allow myself to act on intuition and reconnect with the real me, the soulful me, and the heaven that resides in me.

'There is more to life than the density I had just experienced.'

There is a lighter way to live and I not only have allowed myself to recognize this, more importantly, I have given myself permission to explore, learn and act on this new way of being. To manifest what is Divinely mine. I now frequently tell myself, "Congratulations and welcome back Jill. Thank you for being YOU. Thank you for healing and for wakening. You are needed. Your awakening and awareness is needed." Reading my story is a sign for you to continue exploring. Continue learning and asking questions. Continue opening up to the universal truths that even Jesus taught. Much love to you and much love for your courage.

Tips I want you to consider when facing any situation that may overwhelm you in your daily life:

- Do not look at the whole picture at once. It is overwhelming. Take one area. Set goals as to how you will achieve what you want. How long it will take you to achieve it. Do research and take steps in that direction. Then, take the next area. Repeat the above.
- Focus more on the people who inspire you rather than the people who annoy you. You will get much further quicker in life.
- The strongest factor for success is self –esteem believing you can do it, believing you deserve it, believing you will get it.
- Be sure to do what is right for you. Remember that no one else is walking in your shoes.
- Be brave enough to travel the unknown path and learn what you are capable.
- Think of yourself as a diamond in the rough. How you handle your experiences, and what you learn from them, is how you are 'cut and polished.' Each situation that is resolved with love reveals another beautiful facet of you. Shine on dear ones!
- Forgiveness does not change your past, but it sure changes your present and future for the better.
- Within you is the Power to Rise above any situation or struggle and transform you into the brightest, strongest, version of You, EVER!

With love and gratitude Jill

Karen Oehm

Karen Oehm is a certified Consulting Hypnotist, Life Coach, Traditional-Tibetan Reiki Master, a proud mother of four amazing children, and a truly unique woman that makes you feel comfortable and relaxed, as if you've known her your whole life.

In working with Karen, she will help you come up with a clear and easy plan that fits in with your lifestyle, holding you accountable to make the necessary changes for you to be living the life you've always dreamed about. You'll walk away with a sense of calmness and relief knowing you have someone in your corner, helping direct and support you along the way. She will help you breakthrough old patterns and behaviors so you can live a more balanced life on your terms.

You can reach Karen at:

Website: www.karenoehm.com

Email: ko@karenoehm.com

Open Your Door
By Karen Oehm

Forgiveness is a lifestyle, not an event. We as humans on this planet need to practice forgiveness on a daily basis. It's not a one shot deal. We have to continue to polish our skills in forgiveness and put them into daily practice. How do we do that? Just like with anything, we accomplish this through a process of steps; recognition, release, and then peace.

You cannot obtain peace without going through all of the steps. The most difficult of all the steps, of course, is the first one, recognition. Why is recognition the most difficult step? It means we have to acknowledge that we are not pleased with a person, situation, event, or ourselves.

The last one, ourselves, is the major one we need to be concerned with. Most of us are uncomfortable and do not want to take a good look at ourselves and become aware of how and why we operate the way we do. More importantly, we need to be aware of how we talk to ourselves on a daily basis. Our internal dialogue, self-communication, is extremely important. WE are our own worst enemy by the way we practice, "stinking thinking".

Are you aware of your self-talk? Is it positive or negative? If it's negative, why? What happened to cause you to talk negatively to yourself? Would you allow anyone talk to you the way you talk to you? Do you beat yourself up with your words because there is no one else there to do it and that's what you're used to? Whose voice do you hear when you hear the negative discussions that you cannot turn off in your head?

Did the person really mean what they said the way you interpreted it, or is that YOUR internal dialogue changing the words to fit your perception of yourself?

For example, when I was younger my dad would want me to go grocery shopping with him. So, as with any young teenage girl, I wanted to make sure I looked presentable and would fix my hair and put some makeup on. Well, my dad wasn't a very patient man, especially when it came to girly things. He would always say, "Oh come on, we're not going to a dance or anything, we're just going to the store." Those words always bothered me because they made me feel that I shouldn't take the time for myself. When in reality, my dad probably had other things to do, and just wanted to hurry up and go to the store. My internal language completely turned it around to a negative and processed it as, "Don't take time for yourself, you're not worth it." I had never looked at it in the way that he just wanted to hurry up and go to the store, until writing this chapter. For all of these years I have been carrying around this false belief, and the emotions attached to that self-belief because of MY internal dialogue.

I want to talk about the first step in forgiveness; RECOGNITION. Recognizing the interpretation of words and actions translated to self-talk, recognizing when forgiveness is needed and has occurred. Also, recognizing when we have forgiven and when we haven't. Recognizing our thoughts and emotions attached to the negative memory that needs to be forgiven. There are two parts to this first step.

Part one is recognizing our self-talk and how we interpret what others say to us, which then becomes our internal dialogue. Part two is FORGIVING ourselves! Imagine that! Forgiving ourselves for all of the negative self-talk, self-doubt, self-pity, and self-victimizing! We often don't do that. Instead, we claim to forgive

92

others and sometimes that's easier because it takes our awareness off of us, so we don't have to look at our own faults, insecurities, etc…

Just imagine how free and light we would feel if we were able to forgive ourselves completely!

In our own self-forgiveness we become aware of what true forgiveness really is, and with that comes a new awareness about forgiving others. Remember, forgiveness is a daily practice, we have to constantly be aware of our thoughts and the emotions attached to those thoughts, and our daily conversations with ourselves. Our thoughts become our reality. What we think about, we bring about. With practice, we can learn how to use our self-talk for motivation and not destruction.

Here's an interesting view about thoughts. A thought is neither negative nor positive; it's the emotion attached to the thought that determines if we feel negativity or not. If a thought is thought about long enough, it becomes a belief, and a belief is only a thought you keep thinking. So, in other words, if you continue to tell yourself something long enough, you start to believe it and then it becomes your reality. It can also turn this negativity into your passion and motivation to do and be better than you are today.

We are usually the harborers of a whole bunch of false beliefs, unproductive, untrue thoughts that make up our lives. So how do we change our thought process? Simple, become aware of your thoughts and the emotions attached to those thoughts; are they negative or positive?

As I mentioned earlier, forgiveness is a series of steps. As with anything, taking the first step is usually the hardest, but once we take that first step we start our journey down an amazing path, as long as we continue taking the necessary steps and incorporating them into our daily lives. Inner peace begins the moment you choose not to allow another person or event control your emotions. Well, how do we do that when that person is YOU? Again, that goes back to our thoughts, becoming aware of the emotional attachments, whether negative or positive, to our thoughts on a continual, daily basis.

Why is it difficult to forgive sometimes? You can't give what you don't have. In order to have peace on the outside, you first have to have peace on the inside. Again, this comes back to first forgiving ourselves. We can be our own worst enemies when we haven't forgiven ourselves. There is no one else that can do it for us. We have to be the example to others and emulate what forgiveness is and where it starts. You can do this by working on yourself on a daily basis and showing forgiveness to yourself, and then to others.

> "People often say that motivation doesn't last. Well, neither
> does bathing—that's why we recommend it daily"
>
> —Zig Ziglar

This same principle can be used with forgiveness.

Who do we have to emulate forgiveness? Who do you think of when you think of a person that displays forgiveness?

In my past experiences when I've asked those questions to people, their first thoughts go to people like Jesus, Ghandi, or Mother Theresa. Very rarely have I heard mom, dad, grandparents, or loved ones. Isn't that interesting that there are only a few people that come to mind when it comes to forgiveness, and they are not even remotely related to us? What a shame! What a shame that some people are shocked when someone does something just out of the simple act of forgiveness. It should completely be the other way around; we should be shocked when someone doesn't act out of forgiveness.

My goal in writing this chapter is to influence others to be the self-forgiving, self-loving, and the kind creatures we are meant to be. You need to live and realize that it is a simple process, but we choose to make it difficult. We always have a choice; a choice in our thoughts, a choice in our emotions, a choice in how we process words, a choice in our reactions, a choice in where we operate from; a negative house or a positive house. It's always YOUR choice!!! You define your life by your thoughts, emotions, and choices.

Start living life on your terms and realize that YOU and you alone, are the only one holding the pen to write your script for your movie called LIFE!!! It all starts with a thought!

I challenge you to open your door to the path of forgiveness and start applying the first step; recognition, on a daily basis. Be aware of your thoughts. Be aware of the emotions attached to those thoughts. If they are negative emotions, recognize and acknowledge the feeling, but also, contemplate where those emotions are really coming from and why you feel the way you feel, and ask yourself, is it true?

Once you've done that, it's easier to release the feeling and emotion attached to the thought, getting you one step closer to the ultimate goal of achieving peace and true forgiveness for YOU!

Kelly Walsh

Kelly Walsh, otherwise known as, 'Positivity Princess', is an author, speaker, and friend to all.

After a near death experience following an attempted suicide, Kelly made it her life's mission to share the message she was given, "we are love and we are loved"

 Regardless of color, creed, gender, sexuality, religious beliefs or any other perceived differences we are all one, all connected, all Princes and Princesses of the world and it is time to stand side by side in Global friendship and truly love, care, share.

Kelly has set up the positivity power movement to unite humanity in global friendship. This is a safe haven were people can love, care, and share their life experiences in a loving, safe, and non-judgemental way. Running alongside the positivity power movement is the, 'Love Care Share Foundation,' a charity trust, helping those who live in poverty and suffering around the world.

"The more we LOVE, the more we CARE, the more we SHARE, and together through Positivity Power we change the world!"

Kelly aka Positivity Princess

You can reach Kelly at:

Email: kelly@positivityprincess.com

Website: www.positivityprincess.com

Facebook Group:
https://www.facebook.com/groups/positivitypowermovement/

We Are Love and We Are Loved
By Kelly Walsh

I was a happy child, full of chatter and adventure. This hasn't changed. My obsession with Wonder Woman shaped my calling in life back then.

At the age of ten, my life changed dramatically. My wonderful dad had a breakdown and walked around the house like a zombie. I was scared and confused. Where had my happy, loving dad gone?

During this painful time, I experienced severe bullying at school for being overweight. After knowing how special and beautiful I was, now I started to struggle with low self-esteem. I was outwardly happy with a big smile, but inside I was full of fear, doubt and insecurity.

Five years later I took control of the situation and stopped eating. The weight dropped off and the bullying stopped, but the damage was already done. I had a big smile on my face, but inwardly I was dying. Would I ever learn to truly love and accept myself again?

At nineteen I met my ex-husband while working behind a bar. He was so handsome and I could not believe my luck. How could someone who looked like he did, find ugly me attractive? We fell in love and life appeared to improve. I secured a great job in sales and surprisingly, I excelled in this area, winning numerous awards.

While my sales career flourished, other areas of my life fell apart. I continually searched to fill that missing void deep inside. Since being bullied, I had never really felt accepted and spent many years yearning to be loved and to fit in. Sadly, I missed the realisation that the key to my happiness was deep inside my soul, yearning to come out.

At the age of 33, following years of mental anguish and periods of deep depression, I finally succumbed to my negative self-belief patterns and took a huge overdose. In theory, I should be dead or have severe organ damage, but thankfully I am here with you to share my profound, spiritual experience that has completely changed the course of my life.

While lying in the observation ward with a saline drip attached to my arm, I glanced over the side of my bed and saw a Gideon's Bible. Fear began to envelop me as I pictured myself burning in hell for committing the cardinal sin of attempted suicide. Suddenly a lady with beautiful blonde hair touched my arm and softly said, "When you get out of here read the book, 'Conversations with God' ", and then she vanished. Since then I have been told this book by Neale Donald Walsch comes into your life when it's supposed to. On reflection I believe she was an angel.

Her words, 'when you get out of here,' did nothing to calm me down. I was still extremely fearful and asked to see the onsite minister. He was very kind and caring. As he left he gave me a wooden cross that I held onto for dear life.

The following evening I had my near death experience. It was dark, my eyes were closed and I was feeling anxious. My body was pumping with sweat and I remember having a strong sense of spiritual beings around me. Suddenly I was transported on a journey and could feel myself going through what felt like bumps in the universe. While this was taking place, my whole life flashed before me and I could see and feel the emotions; good, bad, and ugly, associated with my life experience up until then.

This was not a particularly pleasant experience and it felt like a battle to survive. I went through what felt like seven bumps. I have since learnt these bumps are more commonly referred to as dimensions in the universe. After passing through the seventh dimension, I felt the battle was over and a wave of relief surged over me. I was finally at peace and enveloped by unconditional love. It was the most incredible feeling and I wanted to stay lost in that moment forever. In that instant I realised there was no higher source passing judgement on me and the only judgement, when our souls leave our bodies, is the judgement we pass on ourselves. We are love and we are loved.

Suddenly someone spoke to me. I cannot tell you who it was as I have no recollection. In fact it could have just been a voice in this void of love and peace. I was told I was strong, which seemed ironic considering what I had just done. I was told I had a mission to carry out on earth. I was told that as humans we have the capacity to heal physically, emotionally, and spiritually through love. It was demonstrated to me that we are all one, all connected. The voice told me I could be and do anything I wanted.

It seemed like an eternity, as I had no comprehension of time. The following morning I came around from this experience with my arms crossed over my chest and opened them in slow motion. My ex mother in law said I was shouting out about seeing God and angels and I even tried to get out of my bed and escape. I could not understand how I was in a hospital bed after where I had just been. That evening I had a strong sense of the world changing and called out like-minded souls would collaborate to make this happen. I don't think I was taken too seriously as I was in a psychiatric ward. The following week I walked out of hospital with a clean bill of health, which is a miracle in itself.

The time had come to rebuild my life. This was hard because even though I'd had this profound experience, I suddenly started to doubt it. Who would believe me? I put it to the back of my mind and tried my hardest to forget about it. Six months later I met my soul mate and my emotional healing process began. I started to enjoy life, but still suffered periods of deep depression. I now realise it was because I had buried my real truth, living in fear of what others would think of me rather than being my authentic self. When would I learn to become deaf to others and trust my intuition? My heart was yearning for me to act on my soul's purpose, but my head was still in denial.

It took what you might call divine intervention for me to start acting upon the mission I was given. I had been brought up a Methodist, but had stopped going to church in my late teens. Out of the blue I was invited to meet a new friend at a local Pentecostal church. We were greeted at the entrance by a group of young women who asked if I believed in God. I replied that I had a belief in the divine, but I did not fully accept some of what was still being taught in some religious organisations, e.g. God is to be feared and homosexuality is a sin. The service was lovely and at the end I felt as if a thunderbolt had hit me and I began to shake and cry. I decided to explore Christianity further and for the next three months I spent a lot of time with a group of devout Christians who had very strong beliefs about who was going to heaven and who wasn't. This didn't feel right to me. How could a God love unconditionally and yet punish people?

Being in church was the wakeup call I needed. Sermons were being preached about love and forgiveness and yet at the same time I was being told that anyone who was not a practising

Christianity would perish in hell. This was in direct conflict to what I had experienced during my near death experience.

Color, creed, sexuality, religious beliefs, and other perceived differences are irrelevant. We all part of divinities creation, all Princes and Princesses of the world. God, source, universe or whatever resonates with your heart and soul loves and forgives all. It is time for us to stand side by side in global friendship and truly love care share.

Please don't do what I did and keep beating yourself up for past mistakes, holding onto irrational fears, guilt, shame, and negative self-beliefs. Stand tall and proud and see what I see now see in myself and you, a truly special beautiful amazing and unique individual who is capable of changing the world.

Today is the first day of the rest of your incredible life. Stand in front of the mirror and repeat over and over, 'I truly love and forgive myself so that I can truly love and forgive all others.' In doing you will set your heart, mind, and soul free. The ripples of your love and forgiveness will be felt in such a positively powerful way around the world. This is when true healing starts and your incredible journey of self-discovery will really begin.

Time for you to shine your bright light to the world. X

Kirsty Holland

Kirsty is a writer, speaker, and coach, birth doula, out of the box thinker, Master of Change, and a Manifesting Queen!

Originally from the UK, she's been living and loving life in Sunny San Diego, California for the past 9 years.

Kirsty believes we can find the feel-good wherever we are! Whether change has thrown you off course, you are feeling stuck and have no idea how to even begin to take the next step, or you desire to manifest more amazingness into your life, she is here to support you on your journey to co-create your own sunshine!

You can reach Kirsty at:

Email: Grace@graceinthesun.com

Website: www.graceinthesun.com

Facebook: www.facebook.com/graceinthesun

Pinterest: www.pinterest.com/GraceinSD

Instagram: www.instagram.com/graceinthesun

The Day My Whole Life Changed
By Kirsty Holland

The time was 8.20am on Saturday, December 15th 1990. I woke with a jump, startled, slightly disorientated, and with a feeling that something was wrong. My four-week old baby boy, Adam, was asleep in the crook of my right arm. He'd woken a couple of times that night to feed and at 6.15am, I'd brought him into bed to nurse and seemingly drifted off to sleep with him there.

As I looked down at him, I could see something on his face. I looked more closely to find it was a smear of blood that had trickled down from his nose. I realized at that moment something was most definitely wrong. He wasn't breathing. I remember screaming my husband's name frantically, reaching over to him and yelling for him to wake up. I called 999 for an ambulance, as I watched my husband desperately try to breathe life back into our son. Everything seemed to be moving in slow-motion. I was aware that I was making a noise that I have never, ever been able to recreate. An awful wailing sound, like nothing I'd ever heard before. I called my parents while my husband was doing mouth-to-mouth on Adam and we were waiting for the ambulance, desperate for help of some kind, any kind. My dad shared with me, many years later, that one of the most heart-breaking sounds he had ever heard in his life was that of grief; the almost animal-like wails he heard down the phone that morning, and some twenty-one years earlier from my Mum, his wife, when they had woken and found my 9-week old brother dead under very similar circumstances.

The ambulance arrived. I begged them to bring Adam back, to make him breathe. They told me there was only room for one parent to ride with them. As they closed the ambulance doors, I saw my husband watching us leave, his face full of pain. The nine-minute long ride to the hospital, blue lights and sirens blaring all the way, felt endless. They worked on Adam the entire time. We finally arrived at Accident & Emergency, where I was ushered into a side-room by a student nurse as they whisked my new-born son away.

Just minutes later, the same student nurse came back into the room, her eyes red-rimmed and her face obviously damp from recent tears. She asked me if I would like a cup of tea. I politely declined and told her I'd just really like to see my baby, please. She silently left the room.

A few more minutes passed, and she entered the room again. This time with another nurse who was carrying a baby, wrapped in a huge, scratchy, orange hospital blanket. Adam! At last! The nurse holding him looked me in the eye and asked me, 'would you like to hold your son?' She passed my precious bundle to me, turned and left the room. For a second, relief flooded over me. Until I realized that Adam still wasn't breathing, that he was a mottled reddish-purple color on the left side of his face, and that he seemed much heavier, almost by the minute. I looked up in despair, wanting answers, to find the student nurse sat in a chair opposite me, crying. She asked me again, 'would you like a cup of tea, love?'

Grief washed over me. I was in deep physical pain throughout my entire body with hot, swollen, heavy breasts, now engorged and leaking profusely through my clothes because there was no baby to nurse. We were about four hours past the last feed. I stared at my son, trying to make sense of what nobody had the presence of mind to tell me out loud. My baby was dead. My attention turned toward the door as my husband walked in. His face told me that he too had no idea our baby was gone.

What transpired next was a nightmare, as two detectives turned up at the hospital to 'escort' my husband and I to the police station for questioning. It was, apparently, their protocol for any sudden death. Just a few hours after waking on what should have been a typical Saturday morning for a young family with their new baby; my husband and I were separated, taken in police cars to the station, and remained separated while we were interviewed individually by the two detectives. I had a female detective and he had a male. The male detective would come into my interview room and say that my husband had said something and that he, 'wanted to check the details'. Then the female would go into his interview room, with the same tactic. This back and forth between the detectives went on for several hours. We were tired, drained, in shock, had just lost our month-old son, and we were being treated like, and made to feel like, murder suspects. Eventually, we were taken home, where we found a six foot five inch tall uniformed policeman standing outside of our front door. We were told we could go in, but were not allowed to enter our own bedroom as the crime-scene team was removing evidence.

I couldn't make any sense of anything that was going on. I was relieved to find my parents had arrived. After putting the phone down following my call earlier that day, they had immediately driven two hours to be there. The relief turned to pain as I went around my home trying to find any shred of evidence that there had been a baby there just a few hours before. Everything was gone; his clothes, his pram, and the Moses basket, all nowhere to be seen. The door to Adam's room was shut tight. My Mum advised that I leave it closed, that it was for the best. Around that same time, she also called for a home visit from my doctor. He prescribed heavy sedatives and tablets to dry up my still over-abundant milk supply.

The next few weeks were spent waiting in disbelief and grief. On post mortem results, cultures, toxicology reports, on his tiny body being released for burial, and on a cause of death; so much waiting. His funeral was the day before Christmas Eve. The rest of the season passed in a relative blur. My two sisters-in-law were both pregnant at the same time as I was, and had their babies within two weeks of Adam being born. On the news of his death people disappeared, quickly. Friends and family members stopped coming around. My husband and I became more and more distant, while my grief was numbed with Prozac, his became aggression. As the months after Adam's death turned into years, sadly we could never get back to the place of being a carefree, happy young couple again.

There has been so much forgiveness that has taken place and it's a process that has no time limit. Losing my son was my first experience of death. I still had all four grandparents, and had not even lost a pet. I was just 20 years old, still so young, yet forced to grow up quickly to deal with the unimaginable task of burying my first baby. Christmas became impossible for me. Every year I felt held captive in a one-month vigil of remembrance. I was not able to be present fully for myself, or anyone else in my life. I watched as my husband, a proud man from the North of England, struggled with his inability to show emotion; locking himself away behind his pain. Both of us feeling unsupported, battling with guilt and blame, literally drowning in grief; all-consuming and ultimately becoming the downfall of our marriage.

The biggest breakthrough in forgiveness came in understanding there was no blame, or need for guilt. A cause of death of Sudden Infant Death Syndrome (SIDS/Cot Death) leaves parents with many questions. There was no genetic link found to explain the SIDS deaths experienced within my family. To this day, SIDS remains a great mystery to the medical world. What I do know is that finding your way through forgiveness is the key to moving forward. No matter how long it takes. Christmas of 2014 was the first time I felt able to genuinely celebrate. To go out and buy a tree, decorate it, wrap presents, and enjoy the season without the heavy guilt that was oh-so-present in previous years. I'm ok with that because forgiveness has no expiration date.

I will finish with this. If you are going through something similar, please, be gentle with yourself and others, particularly your spouse/partner. We all grieve differently and need to be allowed the space to do that and come to terms with our new reality. Try not to blame each other, but remember all the reasons you fell in love in the first place. Turn toward each other and know that when you find forgiveness and stop blaming, healing will come.

Laraine Sacco

At a very young age, Laraine experienced challenges with speech, issues of being overweight, taunted by bullies, low self-worth, and so much more that all led to eating disorders and a life spiralling downward. She has chosen to embrace the past to rise above gracefully and helps others move forward to a life of purpose and fulfilled destiny.

Laraine enjoys meeting people to create long lasting relationships. She loves spending time with her husband, whom she married over two decades ago, and with their three sons and two dogs. Laraine enjoys quiet time with her family, traveling, exploring, horseback riding, and volunteering to guide young children at their church.

She truly wants to be a light and blessing for others.

You can reach Laraine at:

Email: Laraine@LSacco.com

Phone: 561.373.6856

LinkedIn:
https://www.linkedin.com/pub/laraine-sacco/18/987/b34

Facebook: Laraine Sacco:
https://www.facebook.com/laraine.sacco

Blank Canvas ~ Design the Life You Dream

Is Not Forgiving Someone or Something Imprisoning Your Heart?

By Laraine Sacco

Choosing to Forgive . . .

Unlocks the Cell to the Prison inside your
heart – it sets YOU free!

I Forgive You

Throughout life there is terrible tragedy and it can happen to ourselves or someone we love. As I contemplate life and what needs to be forgiven, it becomes overwhelming. During difficult times, there have been unforgiveable acts done to and by people. As I really think about our time on this earth, the lesson of forgiveness can begin at young age with a hurt so deep it whittles away trust forever. Think about the last time you were hurt or betrayed. Was it by a parent, relative, neighbor, friend, partner, teacher, doctor, or a complete stranger? Pain comes in many forms.

The event is real. It will never go away. It happened. The feeling of humiliation, embarrassment, panic, anxiety, disbelief, fear, confusion, physical and emotional pain, and deep sadness can last what seems like forever because of a series of events or maybe one event. The deep hurt will not last forever, but over time you will learn how to cope and move forward.

The path of life continually changes and affects future generations. The title of the book series, "The Missing Piece" is powerful. What piece is missing for you right now? Forgiving someone, maybe it's you, is very difficult, but it is necessary to be whole. Don't judge. No one will escape. It can be a very dark, frightening world that can and will spin out of control before you can blink an eye. When you are born, the first thing you do is breathe. You are held close to a warm body with a beating heart. You feel love and security. It isn't natural when it is shattered. The pieces are scattered and you don't know what to do or who to trust. How can you begin to heal? The first step is to make a decision to move forward without guilt and forgive not just for yourself, but for the people who love you.

To forgive is giving up resentment, to grant relief, and wipe the slate clean. It is a conscious, deliberate decision to release feelings of resentment or vengeance toward a person or group. It also means to stop wanting to punish someone for an offense or fault.

There are three cases to forgiveness. The first two are the easiest and the last one is more difficult.

1) Offense occurs and the offender realizes it, asks forgiveness, feels regret or remorse, and you accept.

2) Offense occurs and the offender is oblivious. You approach them and the offender realizes what they did. Asks for forgiveness, feels regret or remorse and you forgive.

3) Offense occurs and the offender is oblivious. You approach them and the offender ignores you or worse denies everything and blames YOU!

Which category do you relate to?

What do you do in the third case? You can't forgive because the offender hasn't recognized what they did, asked to be forgiven, and hasn't been regretful or remorseful. The burden is too much to carry with you all the time. How can you forgive and let it go?

Is forgiveness IMpossible?

In Latin, IM means without. Is forgiving the offense or offender without possibility?

Forgiveness is entirely up to you.

There may never be acknowledgement by the offender...ever! It is YOUR heart and YOUR future. Forgiveness is the understanding that people are flawed and can be cruel, harmful, and violent.

Forgiveness is not justification, understanding or explaining the why. It takes time to remove the feelings of hurt, anger, resentment, fear, disbelief, depression, and physical and emotional pain. You have the power to take authority over the offender through loving yourself.

Make the decision to forgive and to let go is recognizing the past and closing that chapter even though the offender is never going to apologize or tell you they are sorry. It's not about them. It's about YOU releasing the chains of negativity and choosing to release the suffering and heavy burden, sorrow, and anguish. Your mind set dictates your moments which creates minutes, hours, and completes the day. Each moment is a choice which starts with a thought.

I'm sure you will agree that so many tragic things have happened to you or someone you know. My story is not about what has happened to me within my world. I can't and won't relive the past. It has been dealt with and let go. I am a compassionate person who worked really hard to be set free! My contribution is to help people understand how to get to the other side. To move past bitterness, anger, depression, anxiety, lack of feeling, lack of purpose, and deep sadness that makes you feel as if you can never be happy and fulfilled again, it starts with YOU. Your mind can create whatever you tell it. Forgiveness is possible. You are capable of reaching happiness as you move further and further away from being a victim. Releasing control and power from the person or situation will set you free. Do not let it define you or your life. It happened. Forgiveness creates healthier relationships, less anxiety, stress, and hostility. Peace will bring lower blood pressure and lower cholesterol levels. Your immune system will become stronger and you will improve the health of your heart. Your heart can be filled with renewed thoughts. Wouldn't that be wonderful?

We all have been affected by pain and suffering at someone else's hand. Horrible things happen to us individually or to people we love. Why? How can human beings be insensitive and feel without regret? This is difficult to understand. As I write this chapter, my heart goes out to those who are suffering. My friend was driving home after bringing her sweet little girl to preschool, excited to be delivering her 3rd child in a week while her 2 year old son was safely strapped in his car seat when an unlicensed, uninsured repeat drunk driver slammed into their car. Life changed. While her unborn son tried to escape her body, she died and so did he. A few weeks later her two year old son joined them in heaven. I've thought about her daughter for 20 years. My thoughts also turn to another mom who didn't see the stop sign because of a change in traffic pattern, rain, fog, and darkness. Her world turned dark that night as she with her family and friends sang hymns raising her children up to God as one by one they passed. Although she was in agonizing pain, she told me her sweet children were with God and will never suffer again. She chose the light. I think about all those who endure verbal and physical abuse, bulimia and anorexia, rape, alcohol, drug, food addiction, the burial of new-born twins, suicides of children and/or a spouse, the suffering or death of a child because of illness, infidelity, homelessness, planes crashing, slaughtering of people, and so much more.

We are born into a reality whether it is of privilege or poverty. Look at children. They smile and giggle. They are amazed at the simplest things in life like the first sign of snow, the beach, a leaf falling from a tree. They are innocent and happy. Life has not changed them. Give yourself permission to smile and giggle once again.

You deserve to be free of turmoil and change your destiny to lift others higher.

"The truth is

Unless you let go,

Unless you forgive yourself,

Unless you forgive the situation,

Unless you realize that the situation is over,

You cannot move forward."

-Dr. Steve Maraboli

"Forgiveness is the attribute of the strong."

-Mahatma Gandhi

In front of you is a blank canvas. It could be blank because of the emptiness within or you can begin to fill it with color. As you move forward through the path of forgiveness think about your future. It's peaceful, loving, happy, calm, bright, open, opportunity to honor yourself and people you love and who love you. What do you see? What color will you gravitate towards? What is your life going to look like? Give yourself permission to forgive, be determined to live, and bless others.

"As I walked out the door toward the gate that would lead to my freedom,

I knew if I didn't leave my bitterness and hatred behind,

I'd still be in prison."

-Nelson Mandela

"Never forget the three powerful resources you

ALWAYS have available to you:

Love, prayer, and

Forgiveness."

Design the Life You Dream

Letisha Galloway

Letisha Galloway is a two time International Bestselling Author. She is an inspirational speaker and the co-author of, 'When New Life Begins: Pushing Past the Old and Embracing the New', 'Family Ties: What Binds Us and Tears Us Apart', and 'The Missing Piece: A Life Transformed'. Letisha authored a book titled, 'Victim to Victor: A Story of Love, Failure and Faith', which chronicles her life as a double leg amputee, domestic violence survivor, losing her only child, and many other events. Letisha is involved in bringing awareness to domestic violence. Additionally, Letisha advocates for the homeless and ending hunger.

You can reach Letisha at:

Email: letisha.nicole@gmail.com

Website: www.letisha.galloway.com

Facebook: www.facebook.com/authorletishagalloway

Twitter: www.twitter.com/letishanicole

LinkedIn:
www.linkedin.com/profile/view?id=239265016&trk=nav_respon
sive_tab_profile

Love Masquerade
By Letisha Galloway

As a teenager I struggled with self-esteem and self-acceptance. I was not confident. I lost my legs as a child and although I always had a smile on my face, I was deeply insecure. Inferiority was at the forefront of my daily thoughts. I searched for love and acceptance, but I felt it was impossible. At the age of 17, I met a 20 year old man who was my dream come true. He said all of the right things. I didn't feel beautiful, but he told me I was.

The relationship went well for several months until I turned 18. Once I turned 18 and was able to visit him as I pleased, the abuse began. It started with him asking me where I was going and when I would return. At times my return time was not early enough for him, so he "suggested" that I return earlier for my safety.

The first time he hit me, I had a delayed reaction. I couldn't believe that the man I loved meant to hurt me. He immediately apologized and I decided to act like the assault never occurred. A few weeks later the second incident occurred. This time he knocked me off of the bed and began choking me. The impact from my head hitting the wall put me into a daze. I wasn't able to defend myself because I was dizzy, and he knew it. As he was choking me, he yelled and told me how everything was my fault, and that if I just listened to him he wouldn't have to hit me.

There were always signs before the abuse began, but not the opportunity for physical abuse as I always had a strict curfew and my friends had to accompany me. I stayed because I didn't think I deserved better. I thought that once I lost him no one else would want me. I wanted to change him back into the man I met in the beginning. I tried to love the abusive ways out of him. I truly believed that if I was a good girlfriend and did what he asked, he would stop beating me. I made excuses for him. I gave myself many reasons of why I should stay. Every time I was about to leave, he apologized and I accepted it. I reasoned that everyone makes mistakes and he said he was sorry. I told myself that the last time he hit me would be the very last time because he loved me and just lost his temper.

After our relationship ended, I continued the pattern of not loving myself. I married a man who did not respect me or himself enough to remain faithful. I entered a few unhealthy romantic relationships. I didn't realize that I was abusing myself by accepting the outside abuse. Abuse was all I knew. It was what I was accustomed to. I didn't know what it was like to be in a loving relationship. Love was a foreign concept to me. Having a healthy relationship was not the norm for me. When a man treated me nicely I didn't know how to respond. I didn't know how to love anybody because I didn't love myself. I was a broken person searching for the missing pieces.

With each relationship, my low self-esteem continued to plummet. The abusive relationships damaged my view of relationships. Before a man could take me on a third date, I would find a way to sabotage it. I decided that a nice man could not possibly be kind hearted, no he would later change into someone evil. I was not willing to risk being hurt again. I decided that it was better to stop dating early, rather than risk getting hurt later. Men would often ask me what they did wrong and if I would reconsider. I would say that I wasn't ready for a relationship and wish them luck. The truth was that I wanted a relationship, but was not willing to open my heart to receive the love I desired. By not opening my heart and keeping up my defences, I cheated myself out great opportunities to build lasting relationships with people who had no ill will towards me.

Now that I am older, I realize how truly unfair I was to myself and the men who tried to form loving relationships with me. I didn't give any of them a real opportunity. I held what my abusers did to me against men who had never done anything wrong. Not only did the abuse affect my dating relationships, it affected my overall quality of life. I wasn't able to give my family and friends the best part of me because I was angry and resentful towards my abuser. At times someone would say, "good morning," and I would reply, "It's just morning". I talked negatively to myself every day. I told myself that no one else would want me and that my abuser was right. For a long time I gave my abuser power over my life. I didn't realize that he still had the power years after we stopped dating. By not forgiving him I relinquished the power over my life. Holding on to the past and the hatred associated with it, kept me in an emotional prison. Set yourself free by forgiving others.

Forgiving others does not mean that you must be their friend again or even call them. Forgiveness means that you hold no ill will towards them. It means that you are able to move on with your life regardless of who mistreated you because you know your worth.

I forgave my abuser. The road to forgiveness was not without tears. I have found that tears are sometimes a necessary part of the journey to healing. The journey was necessary for me to heal enough for me to let love into my life again. Forgiveness has opened my life to new possibilities. I am now able to see each person for who they are. I do not penalize them for mistakes they have not made. Each person deserves to be seen for who they really are. In the past I wasn't able to give people that opportunity.

Forgiving those who have hurt you will not always be an easy process. Some people still ask me today how I was able to forgive my abuser. It was not an easy process. There were times when I wasn't sure forgiveness was possible. It seemed like an impossible task to forgive someone who inflicted so much pain physically and emotionally. I was able to forgive my abuser when I forgave myself.

Forgiving yourself is the ultimate expression of self-love. God forgives us daily. If he can forgive us daily for our mistakes, we should be able to forgive ourselves too. Forgiving yourself frees you from the bondage that others try to put you in by holding your past mistakes against you. Forgiving others allows you to break free from the bondage of having hatred or unresolved hurt in your heart from what others have done to you. When you withhold forgiveness you allow the person who hurt you to keep power over your life. The anger and resentment that you feel towards them will continue to negatively impact your relationships and the overall quality of your life.

Forgiving myself was the missing piece in me being able to have the inner peace that I desired. I searched everywhere for the missing piece. I didn't realize that I had the missing piece the entire time. I had the ability to forgive myself. Forgiving myself has allowed me to experience a level peace that I have never experienced.

Tips:

1. **Forgive others**

   In order to live a truly peaceful life you must forgive others. A productive life is not possible when you are carrying around hatred and withholding forgiveness. The lack of forgiveness is not unlike a disease that will spread to other areas of your life. It not only affects those that have hurt you, but it affects those who you cherish. The people you cherish do not receive the best you possible because of the hurt and anger in your heart. When we refuse to forgive others and ourselves we rob ourselves of inner peace. Forgiveness allows us to live the life God intended. He intended for us to always be free and to have peace within.

2. Forgive yourself

Forgiving yourself is the key to living an abundant life. Forgiveness is not only for others it is for you. Many times we hold on to our past mistakes and punish ourselves. The negative self-talk has to stop. You are worthy of forgiveness. Speaking words of encouragement over your life will help you to forgive yourself. Forgiving yourself is a freeing experience. When you forgive yourself it won't matter how often others try to hold your past mistakes against you.

Lil Lezarre

Lil Lezarre, co-author of seven bestsellers, entrepreneur, professional speaker, and transformation guide, shares her story of how the pain endured during an abusive marriage and ugly divorce, including being alienated from her kids, transformed her in to the confident, giving person she is today. Through her experiences, Lil became very clear on her true values, shed her limiting beliefs, and is now living her life with total contentment. Grateful for all she has learned about herself through the terrible times, Lil's greatest joy is having reclaimed a loving relationship with her three children, enhanced by the happiness that comes from guiding others to a better sense of self.

You can reach Lil Lezarre at:

Website: www.lillezarre.com

Twitter: Lil Lezarre

Email: lil.lezarre@gmail.com

Facebook: Lil Lezarre

LinkedIn: Lil Lezarre

Forgiveness – It's Not What You Think

By Lil Lezarre

We typically think forgiveness is about the other person, but really it has nothing to do with them, it is all about us and our feelings inside. The Webster's Dictionary states, 'to stop feeling anger toward (someone who has done something wrong): to stop blaming (someone)'. In the end this is what you want to feel, but for some reason we interpret it to say, 'we're OK with what they've done'. We can stay stuck with that burning hatred towards them inside and it can ruin our lives.

My definition, realizing the lessons you have learned from all of your trying times and applying them to make you an amazing person on the inside because of all these lessons, you can see others with understanding and compassion and be very clear on the kind of person you want to be. Our past serves only to give us experience, learn from it and grow.

You have a choice and yes, it's very hard to get rid of that anger for what they've done to you, but when you start focusing on yourself, rebuilding yourself on the inside, and growing from your experiences, you start becoming proud of yourself and the wonderful person you are. You realize that it's not your fault this happened. You can look in the mirror and love the person you're looking at. Unfortunately, there are bad people in this world and you know firsthand what the signs of a toxic person are. You have the choice to remove all toxic people from your life. You have the choice to do the things that make you happy. You can make yourself the priority without guilt. It's all up to you and only you.

At the age of 16, I ran away from home with my ex-husband and 22 years later I ran away again, but this time with my three children into a women's shelter. There was always emotional abuse towards me, but when it started turning physical on the kids (spankings), I had to do something. His jealousy was escalating; I couldn't even hug the kids in front of him. Till this day I know that we wouldn't be alive if we hadn't escaped.

It was never my intention to hurt him and when I left I tried making it as easy on him as possible. I left him with pages of detailed instructions on how to run our business. I even took the older vehicle and only what we needed to start again. Those first few days after we left, I felt terrible for the pain he must be feeling. When dealing with my lawyer, I kept asking myself if I was lying, my story seemed so terrible, but every time I reviewed my affidavit it was all true, I made sure I didn't exaggerate about anything.

He didn't see the kids for six months because I would allow supervised visits only and it was up to him to arrange it. We started with supervised, then unsupervised and it didn't take long for his manipulations on the kids to influence them and eventually all three chose to live with him. He told the kids it was my fault our perfect family life was over; I was a slut; I took all the money and stashed hundreds of thousands of dollars away; I didn't love them, I only wanted them for the tax deduction. He encouraged the kids to look through my closet and when they found the bag with their baby teeth from the tooth fairy and my emergency candles for a power failure, he told them I was practicing demonic ceremonies; one of the reasons my daughter was worried about moving back with me was her instilled fear that she might be molested by my new partner and that we might have cameras mounted in our shower; and the list goes on. I never blamed the kids, they were young and being manipulated by someone they trusted, their father. It killed me to watch this, but there was nothing I could do. Even our court system fell for his 'poor me' story, giving him primary residency.

My daughter lived with her dad for less than a year before returning back to me. The boys lived with him for five and eight years and wouldn't have anything to do with me. I called them every year on their birthday to say, 'I love you and my door will always be open for you – when you choose'. I felt so cheated, I knew I was doing the right thing, but at every turn I was getting knocked down. Counseling sessions, support groups and my Naturopath were my life savers and I worked very hard on myself for years. I even got my Level 1 Reiki to help me deal with the pain. During this time I definitely felt a 'burning' inside. I hated him for what he was doing, especially to the kids, using these innocent beings. I was always in reaction mode.

In 2010, I started, 'Tender Loving Cups,' when I saw there was a need for a service which provided properly fitting quality bras at affordable prices. I started my company from scratch while working at a fulltime job. That was the year my daughter moved in with her dad and I wanted to be so busy I couldn't feel my pain.

I was also very active with the, 'Alpine Club of Canada' (ACC). Having discovered my passion for our Canadian Rockies, the ACC gave me the opportunity to learn new leadership skills at affordable prices. I'm regularly in the mountains hiking, camping, rock and ice climbing, and skiing. Discovering what you love to do and doing it regularly is crucial for your growth on the inside. You will meet like-minded people and your confidence will soar as you discover you can do anything you want to.

Start listening to your gut; it talks to you all the time. When you get that uneasy feeling inside, that's your body telling you something isn't right. You will always do the right thing, even if it means it's to learn from a lesson. The key is to learn and grow.

You may need help to grow, hire a professional and don't stop looking till you find the one that resonates with you, the one you feel totally comfortable telling everything to. Trust your instincts. The more you listen to your gut, the louder it will speak to you.

I realize now that without going through those hard times, I never would have worked so hard on rediscovering myself. Nothing happens without action, you have to actively work at it. You have to make yourself priority, surround yourself with positive and supportive people. As you build yourself from the inside, you will find you're feeling better about yourself. Once you start realizing that they are assholes and there's nothing you can do about that, it's their problem, you will start letting go. Since we have kids together, I still have to occasionally deal with him and it is a constant battle for me. Every time he pulls one of his stunts I have to take a step back and refocus on me. I still struggle with getting mad at myself for letting him get to me, but it's shorter lived every time. I no longer have that burning inside.

All that hard work has paid off as now I see others with empathy. In 2014, I discovered my purpose, to help others. I developed my 'PTDS' program (Post Traumatic Divorce Self). I know how to survive these trying times and I share my advice and guide others through their hell. I co-authored in seven international best-selling books. I also discovered meditation and do it daily and through meditation I've realized the power of the Universe and the, 'Law of Attraction'. What you put out there definitely comes back.

Honesty, authenticity, respect, and gratitude are values that are huge to me and are my priority for my business and personal life. You must have success on the inside before you can truly have success on the outside.

I am thrilled to report that all three kids are back in my life and I have the most amazing relationship with all of them. They have figured out their dad and respect me for everything I've done. They also share my passion for our mountains and we are becoming a family again.

I wouldn't change a thing about my life and I'm very proud of the person I've become. I am happy on the inside. I'm clear on my priorities and values and enjoying every moment. This clarity is because of what I've learned from my past, from my lessons, and all my hardships. This is about you and only you, it has nothing to do with the other person. Forgiveness releases you from your past.

Lisa Beane

Lisa Beane, International Best Selling Published Author and Board Certified Integrative Nutrition Health Coach.

Lisa's story of ill health and mandatory behavior change at 46 were the inspiration in forming, 'BeaneNATURAL.' She bridges the gap between traditional medicine and holistic health via lifestyle intervention.

Through Lisa's guidance, you'll learn to open up your mind and find clarity in seeing your possibilities; to which are the solution you have within you.

Walking away with improved confidence, you will be empowered to become the healthiest, happiest, and best version of you.

Lisa's work globally includes:

Coaching

Virtual/Live Retreats

Motivational/Educational Workshops

Speaking Engagements

You can reach Lisa at:

Email: lisa@beanenatural.com

Facebook: www.facebook.com/lisa.a.beane

Facebook: www.facebook.com/Beanenatural

Website: www.beanenatural.com

LinkedIn: www.linkedin.com/pub/lisa-beane/19/122/325

Holistic Health Turned My World Upside Down

By Lisa Beane

It was May of 2009, my doctor told me for the third time that year, "Lisa, I don't know why you are still feeling so bad, you're on the best medication there is," then he handed me yet one more prescription. One more drug to add to my increasing number of pharmaceuticals to be taken daily. One more notch in my belt of drugs that has been matched to my symptoms. If I fill this prescription, I will be taking approximately thirteen different pharmaceuticals, daily. If I fill this prescription, will it release my pain and will it allow me to go back to work? If I fill this, still one more prescription, will it leave me with additional new symptoms, mere witnesses to the crime?

I left the office hopeless, fearful, crying, and with no future in sight of going back to work or feeling better anytime soon. The pain and exhaustion had been unbearable for so long that a year prior to this visit, I resigned from my career, as I was no longer able to carry out my duties of travel, managing clients, and representatives without slipping discs in my lower spine and without being in a constant and tremendous amount of pain and exhaustion. I was 47 years old and my doctor didn't know what to do with me, nor did any specialist. My body was screaming with every move I made, with every drug I took, and it was telling me to find a better way.

Is it possible that each drug was a Band-Aid for my symptoms and each drug created more symptoms? This sounds like a no-win situation. My symptoms of fibromyalgia pain, adult onset of pre-diabetes, adult onset of asthma, lupus, and Epstein Barr symptoms, acute inflammation, severe headaches, chronic sinusitis and bronchitis, chronic fatigue, IBS, rheumatoid arthritis symptoms, allergies that multiplied year after year, high blood pressure, hypothyroid symptoms, pelvic floor dysfunction, PMS symptoms, candida, interstitial cystitis symptoms, incontinence, irregular sleep habits, chronic cough, and excessive mucous all left me and the medical world bewildered for quite some time. Everyone remained confused because there were very few answers, instead an increasing number of symptoms and prescriptions written.

It appears the medical community is trained in how to treat symptoms, maintain ill health and not fix the underlying cause of the matter. There is a certain amount of financial support that is needed to keep Big Pharma in business. Without physicians prescribing drugs to their patients, there would be no Big Pharma. Have you ever known a family member or friend to improve their health to the point of no longer needing high blood pressure drugs, diabetic medication, and cholesterol drugs without undergoing a major lifestyle change? Have you ever asked a physician how much nutrition education they received in Medical School? Traditional doctors do not have the time or the training to educate on healthy eating, toxins, balance, mind, body, and spirit. They don't have the time because our insurance companies are dictating the minutes that physicians spend with a patient. It is my observation that they are taught to focus strictly on the symptom, matching a drug to it, and not on the entire body as a whole. My experience is that once a new symptom or diagnosis is determined, a drug is given to match that ailment or diagnosis, and there is never an opportune time to be able to come off of those drugs.

Medical Schools only accept top of class students. Of course, these students must be brilliant to be able to learn much about the human body. A curriculum was created many, many moons ago to teach medical students to become a great doctor. Seemingly, this particular education hasn't been able to keep up with the continually evolving dis-ease over time. Who ever heard of autoimmune disease 50 and 100 years ago?

My entire career revolved around doctor offices, hospitals and the medical world. I believed in the doctors that I worked for, as well as those I entrusted with my own medical care. I had a tremendous amount of faith in physicians and their education, as I continued to make appointments with them. I did this without question, because that is what I was conditioned to do. The media does an excellent job to advertise the amazing current and new prescription drugs that we are encouraged to ask our doctors about. They have all the answers to our illnesses and could prescribe the perfect drug for me. Even though each prescription drug always, always, always comes with multiple and serious side effects, I was raised and trained that the doctors know what they are talking about and would help me. I respected doctors as authoritative figures.

Holistic health turned my world upside down, in a favorable way. I discovered that by reversing my gut damage, and increasing the nutrients my body would now use and not dismiss, getting my thyroid burning optimally, eating good quality food free from toxins and chemicals, stopping all prescription drugs, releasing toxic waste from my body via holistic measures, and removing toxins from my home and life, I would absolutely be able to gain my quality of life back. Taking a holistic approach, I no longer have to rely on the countless prescription drugs daily, to ease my symptoms. Through lifestyle changes I was able to release the pain, the inability to have quality of life at such a young age and I found myself alive and able to go about everyday living, as I once knew it.

Has a physician ever recommended you stop eating sugar and simple carbs as refined sugar? Have they ever said sugar is addictive and has a heroine effect on the body? Have they ever recommended to you to stop drinking cow's milk because it is full of mucous, hormones, antibiotics, and the inhumane treatment of the animal increases their cortisol levels? Has anyone ever suggested that you not purchase food that is processed, packaged, prepared, and full of antibiotics, preservatives, hormones, and GMO's? Instead, purchase whole fresh food and experiment with food that is free range, grass fed, wild caught and strictly organic.

Why should I forgive the medical community for not being able to help me? After all, feeling bitter and disappointed was much easier than trying to forgive. As my body began to reverse its illnesses through a holistic approach, I quickly discovered that not forgiving would keep my body at a juncture of brokenness, as it maintains a state of disease. Forgiveness is an act of setting myself up for vulnerability, opening myself up to more pain. I also learned that without releasing the pain of being hurt, our bodies hold on tight to that and will allow ourselves to stay in a world of physical and emotional residual.

Forgiving the medical profession has allowed me to open up my mind to other possibilities, ways of reversing illnesses and getting off of multiple drugs. It has allowed me the freedom to make choices. It has opened my eyes up to how medicine has helped my illnesses progress and how stopping all drugs and taking a holistic approach has helped my health improve.

This amazing journey has led me to becoming an, 'Integrative Nutrition Health Coach' and International Best-Selling Author. I empower women who want to make a lifestyle change and increase their quality of life. We only get one opportunity to live this life, in this body and I choose to live the second half of my life more educated about my own health and share my knowledge with the world.

I want to leave you with this message. It is not my intention to bash or criticize traditional medicine. There have been many brilliant physicians and amazing prescription drugs in the history of this world. We will always need certain pharmaceuticals such as pain medication and antibiotics, as well as hospitals, doctors, specialists, and surgeons. People will need to have procedures, bones get broken, and blood needs to be transfused. Emergency, medical, and surgical care is inevitable. There is a viable need for both traditional medical care and integrative nutrition. Sadly, our doctors are not trained in what it will take to reverse illness and what it will take to gain and maintain excellent health through proper nutrition. Physicians are taught to match a drug to a symptom and be content with the patient taking this drug forever!

Please note that I am not a physician or doctor of any kind. I am a woman who simply took her health into her own hands. It was NOT at the advice of any medical practitioner that I decided to stop all prescription drugs, including prednisone, in a split second. I do not recommend anyone do this as a result of reading my story. It could be dangerous to your health. Always seek out the guidance of your physician.

In my heart of all hearts, I truly forgive the Western Medical world. They don't know what they don't know!

Maxine Browne

Maxine Browne's simple step-by-step process will keep you focused as you move from your passion to a self-published book through her workshops and coaching program.

Maxine co-authored the International Best Sellers, 'The Missing Piece' and 'The Missing Piece in Business.' She is the author of 'Years of Tears', and 'Cinderella's a Fella: He's Nobody's Princess.'

She is also a social justice activist, focusing on women's issues such as healthy relationships, co-parenting, and rebuilding your life after divorce or other setback. She empowers people to live their best life.

You can reach Maxine at:

Website: www.maxinebrowne.com

Facebook: www.facebook.com/maxine.browne.792

Twitter: www.twitter.com/maxinebrowne

Freedom through Forgiveness
By Maxine Browne

Those years were so confusing. He said he loved me.

He told me that our blended family would have a happy ending. I believed him.

He didn't tell me he was still married when he married me.

He didn't tell me he would call me names or cut me off from those I loved.

He didn't tell me he would try to control the very air I breathed,

But he did.

I believed him. I defended him. I sided with him.

There were many crossroads, and I turned towards HIM (and away from other people, places, and things) every time.

Like when I told my friends to leave me alone because he said they were using me.

Like when I told my children to obey him to keep him from being angry.

Like when I sided with him against my only sibling and her husband.

He didn't tell me he deceived me,

But he did.

After 10 years of mind-numbing, eye-blinding manipulation, lies and control, I got out. I was finally free.

I found myself in a maddening, no-holes-barred, blinding rage. I was like a poison-spewing fountain that vomited my anger onto everyone. I cursed (didn't used to), had problems with authority figures (didn't used to), and trusted NO one (didn't used to).

My life was a mess. I was fighting for freedom, wildly punching the air, but no one was there. Why was I spending every moment fighting ghosts?

I decided the only way to be free from my past was to forgive my abuser and to forgive myself. I had no idea how.

I was amazed how easy it was to forgive my abuser. Perhaps it was easy because I had forgiven others before him. I can't say. I knew if I ever wanted this individual to live outside of my personal space, I had to forgive him and let him go, forever. This happened within 1 ½ years of leaving him.

The most difficult part of my journey has been forgiving myself. I don't know how you feel, but I always felt I was a good judge of human nature. However, this man had gotten to the most vulnerable places imaginable and had torn them to shreds. No one had ever made my children a target before. I mean, who would do that? I never saw it coming, and when I was in the thick of it, couldn't see through the smoke and mirrors of the holograms he was projecting. I bought his illusion and I believed him.

Who would believe a man who said…

My children were disrespectful (okay, maybe),

My daughter was not stable and perhaps even dangerous (doubtful),

Everyone was against us because of our religious beliefs (highly doubtful).

But I did…

Who can imagine that I would allow…

Him to separate me from my children,

Him to abuse my children,

Him to drive my children from our home,

But I did…

When I took off my Rose Colored Glasses and looked at the facts, I could hardly believe what I was seeing. An outsider would have said that…

I had abandoned my children,

I had neglected my parents as they aged,

I had surrendered financial control to my husband,

I let it happen.

And I did

My life looked like the blast site of an atomic bomb. There was nothing left of my former self and the things I once held precious. I couldn't believe it. How had I allowed this? How could I ever recover all I had lost?

I decided to choose life. What did that look like? I had to forgive myself. After all, how could you create a foundation unless you cleared the rubble of the past? Can you imagine New York trying to build a structure on top of the rubble of 9/11? No way, right? They first had to haul away the debris before they could build something new.

I believe the only pathway to freedom is to accept 100% responsibility 100% of the time. That is the only way we hold the power of choice so we can set the course for our lives. As painful and as horrific as it appeared, I had to accept 100% responsibility for all that had happened and the pain it caused. If I blamed him, I gave away my future. That was not an option. My future belonged to me, and I decided to fight for it.

Today I understand that back then I didn't know. I didn't even know what I didn't know about what I didn't know. I had built my life on a belief that people say what they mean and mean what they say. Deceit of this magnitude was foreign to me. It was a life lesson. I forgive myself for my past ignorance.

I believed the lies I was told. The decisions I made based on those lies created catastrophic consequences for me and for my children. I had to accept responsibility for the decisions I made, as well as the consequences of those decisions. Today, I forgive myself. Since the consequences had an impact on my children, I had to ask my children for their forgiveness also.

My children forgive me and take it back on a regular basis. Although it hurts when they are angry with me yet again, if it is based on their past pain, there is nothing more I can do after I have asked for their forgiveness. That is my part. The rest is their healing journey and their own struggle to forgive their mother for the pain she caused them.

A healthy choice for me has been choosing to live a life firmly rooted in the present and the future. The past has taught me things, and, for that, I am grateful. However, I spend little time ruminating. I find myself too busy living for that.

Tips for the Reader:

Some people never take the leap of faith to forgive. That decision handcuffs them to a past and to someone who no longer thinks about them. You can make a different choice. It is up to you. Use the key of forgiveness to set yourself free.

Did you believe something you later discovered to be untrue? We all do that. Forgive yourself.

Did someone you trusted blatantly lie to you? I understand how you may blame yourself for believing their lies. However, were *you* lying? No! Therefore, you need to acknowledge that at that moment you did not know what you know now. How can you blame yourself for a learning curve? So, forgive yourself. It's okay or, even if you don't think so, it will be okay one day.

Know that forgiveness is a process. It has stages. Whatever stage you are in right now is the perfect one. Forgiveness is a journey. We can get there by taking one step at a time.

Michelle Stacy

Welcome to the world of Michelle Stacy. She is beginning a new phase in her writing career with this contribution to, 'The Missing Piece' series. Michelle is an online freelance writer, instructor, mentor, and coach. She holds a degree in Psychology, is a Broad Certified/State Licensed Massage Therapist, CranioSacral Therapist, Reflexologist, Certified Yoga Instructor, a Licensed Realtor, and a wife and mother of five. Michelle also works in marketing and sales. She views her entire life as a research phase that has led up to this turning point in co-authoring an International Best-selling Series.

Through her experience and educational background, Michelle has kept her focus on her family and helping others achieve success.

Plans for the future include sharing more throughout her writing. She looks forward to touching each one of you in a special way.

You can reach Michelle at:

Website: www.mymichellestacy.com

Finding Strength in Forgiveness
By Michelle Stacy

Forgiveness is an ongoing process. Sometimes I don't realize when I am holding onto something that needs forgiveness. Acknowledging this can be most difficult. Of course saying the phrase, "I forgive you," or, "Please forgive me," can feel like swallowing a watermelon whole. Three simple words hold so much meaning…

I will never forget the day. It was a day that began a journey for me into turmoil of emotions, pain, insecurity, resentment, denial, and eventually reconciliation and forgiveness. This particular day I was sitting in a psychology class at college. My boyfriend sat next to me. The instructor was lecturing on the five stages of grief. It was hot outside and the windows were open. There was a bug crawling across my notebook. Deep into the explanation of denial, it hit me. I looked up from the fascinating bug and with tears in my eyes spoke out loud, "Oh crap. I've been in denial all these years?"

What a powerful realization for me.

You see it all goes back to when I was eleven. While I didn't fully understand the events happening around me, I knew it was bad. My mom was upset. My brothers wouldn't talk much more than uttering a few words. I was dropped off at school instead of riding the bus. I had a math test. I was good at math, but none of the skills were with me on that morning as I sat with a blank paper.

At recess, my teacher kept me inside and asked me what was wrong. I told her. My father was in the hospital.

Ok, so my father was in the hospital, but what did that mean? I wasn't sure. After school I was picked up by a family member and taken to the hospital. My mother and brothers were already there. I wondered why they were allowed to be at the hospital when I had to go to school. In the waiting room I still felt like I was kept in the dark. I heard words like heart and surgery and recovery time. I asked for my mom. When she came to the waiting room she told me I didn't want to see my father like he was. I pleaded to see him. I didn't want to stay in that waiting room by myself. It was boring and smelled funny. When she agreed she told me just for a minute.

In my father's room, I didn't know what to say. He was in a bed and had all this stuff hooked up to him. Nobody told me what it was all doing there. Nobody explained to me what it all meant. Everyone there was quiet and not talking. After a few short minutes my mom took me back to the waiting room where my aunt was waiting to take me back to her house. The next several days I went straight to my aunt's house after school. The idea was that it would be easier for me to have somewhere else to be. I could play, talk, do my homework, and not have to be sitting in the smelly waiting room or the scary ICU room where my father lay in a coma; hooked up to machines and with large tubes and small tubes with needles.

What really happened was I heard nothing, saw nothing, knew nothing. When my mom picked me up from my aunt's house each day, she was tired and just wanted to get home. I had no news of my father's condition. I had no interaction with my family. They thought it was best for me to have some distance from the situation. My mom didn't want me to remember my father like he was lying in that hospital bed. I was afraid to ask questions. I knew nobody would answer me truthfully anyway.

The next week was a blur. My father did not recover. There was a funeral. It went by quickly. There were lots of crying people and food that I didn't want to eat. I was tired of people trying to hug me and ask me how I was doing. During the weeks following the funeral, I retreated to my bedroom most of the time and away from it all.

What happens after the funeral? What happens when all the sad people go back to living their own lives and stop bringing you food? What happens the day after, when you have to go back to life as you now know it?

I'll tell you what happens. What happens is you move through your day somewhat like a zombie. You go to school. You take that next math test. You eat lunch, play with your friends, and come home. You tell yourself everything is fine. You tell yourself that Dad is at work, out in his garage, or with the guys. You tell yourself you will see him tomorrow. You tell yourself whatever you need to get through this day and on to the next.

You tell yourself these things over and over again until you find yourself sitting in a class 10 years later and hear that one word that makes you snap: Denial. It hit me like an anvil hits Wile-E-Coyote. When I spoke up in the middle of my instructor's lecture all eyes turned to me. Just as quickly, I excused myself from class with my boyfriend on my heels. Not knowing what I was going to do, he took me for coffee and we talked about my revelation. He held me while I processed ten years' worth of denial. Beyond realizing that my father was not going to come home any day now, I had a bigger set of feelings to deal with. Why had my mother kept me from experiencing the same things she allowed my brothers to experience? Why I was the only one sent off to my aunt's house, and to school, and had the chance to see my father only one brief moment in the hospital? Why was I singled out as the one who couldn't handle daily updates on my father's condition; only to sneak snippets of adult conversations?

Finally, what ramifications took place as a result of being excluded? In the years after my father's death I had feelings of insecurity, distancing myself, intimacy issues, needing a male role model, being an outsider, not being smart enough, and not trustworthy. I'm sure I could go on.

How do I heal from the loss of my father, dealing with it a decade after it happened? Well, as hard as it was to face, I needed to talk to my mother. I needed to find out why she thought it best to keep me separate from the rest of my family at such a pivotal point in all of our lives. I needed for her to know how that affected me and still affected me years later. Of course she did the best she could at the time and in her opinion the best for me was to have me someplace comfortable instead of being at such a scary and sad (and smelly) hospital while my father's condition deteriorated each day. She was trying to protect me from the memory of seeing my father that way. She had no idea how I bottled it all up and tucked the whole thing in the back of my heart and mind.

Hearing my mother explain the why's of her decisions through tears gave me the closure I needed. Knowing her side of it gave me the strength to forgive the resentment I felt. I forgave my mother for excluding me. I was able to forgive my brothers for being privileged to sit by her side while I was sent away. I was able to understand how their pain differed from mine. I still struggle with the insecurity and feelings of being excluded, but I have come a long way and will continue to work on it.

Forgiving the events that week my father lost his final battle, and the years of denial afterwards allowed me to move forward. I saw a brighter side to my future. I felt uplifted and not weighted down with the heaviness of unshed grief. Forgiving did not change the past, but opened up the ability for new memories of that time of my life. Talking with my family allowed me to retrieve some good moments I had clumped together and blocked with my denial. Forgiving showed me my strength.

"The weak can never forgive. Forgiveness is the attribute of the strong."

- Mahatma Gandhi

Nicky Marshall

Nicky Marshall is an Author, Mentor, Speaker, and CEO/Founder of, 'Discover Your Bounce Ltd.'

In 2010, Nicky suffered a stroke after a diving accident. Thanks to her knowledge in meditation, positive thinking, intuition, and holistic therapies, she healed her body and mind. Within 3 years she was fit to dive, well, and happy.

Nicky is a change maker, an inspirer, and a good listener. Nicky has 5 books in publication with 3 more in the pipeline. Combining her management accounting knowledge, knack for stress-busting and infectious laugh Nicky is a favorite with entrepreneurs aiming for success.

You can reach Nicky at:

Website: www.discoveryourbounce.com

Facebook: www.facebook.com/discoveryourbounce

Facebook: www.facebook.com/nickymarshallauthor

Twitter: www.twitter.com/bounce2success

YouTube:

https://www.youtube.com/channel/UCBXK2Ut7IyL39-Pc1cRr2lA

The Importance of Being Stubborn
By Nicky Marshall

Sitting on the floor of our living room was a great place to do some thinking. I had sat here quite a bit in the last 3 days, sometimes thinking and sometimes just letting the multitude of thoughts wash over me. At times, my sadness and fear gripped my stomach and yet there was this enduring peace throughout my time pondering the meaning of my life.

Not so long ago life had been at full speed. I had just opened my lifelong dream business, a holistic coffee shop called, 'The Witches Brew'. We had a friendly, welcoming coffee shop at the front and two beautiful therapy rooms at the back. I had been so proud on opening day, welcoming in family, friends, and new customers.

Over time though, the reality of six days a week with very little help set in. I would be up at 5am writing newsletters and marketing materials before heading into the shop to open up. After a busy day making teas and coffees and serving lots of cake we would close, then within half an hour I would see my therapy clients or run evening events.

Once home, I would gratefully eat the meal my wonderful husband had prepared. Usually I would eat alone as his 5am start meant he would usually be in bed by 9pm. No bed for me though, I checked through e-mails, processed event bookings, and wrote the ever increasing to do list for the next day.

Quite frankly there is only so long a body can go on living on coffee, cake, and late night dinners. My background in holistic therapy had taught me this. I didn't know how to make a change though and assumed I could do this for a while longer. How wrong I was!

A routine day of scuba diving ended with a coastguard rescue, two ambulance trips and 14 hours of recompression treatment. I suffered a muscular, skeletal, and cerebral bend (or DCI). Nitrogen bubbles lodged in my brain meant I suffered a stroke. I was 40 years old.

Initially the enormity of my situation hadn't sunk in at all. After two weeks of rest, I was back to work, convincing everyone it was business as normal. I tried to keep the same hours and level of activity as I had previously done, however my body had other plans.

I could hardly use my left hand, my once dextrous fingers now sat curled up and forcing them open hurt. I had no strength in my arm and lifting anything was a challenge.

My left leg felt unreal and I doubted its ability to keep me upright. I had no co-ordination of the clutch and accelerator while driving so endlessly stalled even on the short journey to work.

My memory was patchy and mid-sentence a word I was just about to use would get stolen away leaving my mind with a completely blank space

My arm ached constantly and I just felt so, so tired.

Months of struggling had led me to the living room floor and now I had no plan, no energy, and no zest to know where to go next.

During those hours, my mind wandered to closing the doors on my business. I had chatted with friends over the last few days and they had all agreed. No-one would think me a failure if I shut the shop, my accident had come at a critical time for a new business, and it would be easier to give in and close.

I just wanted my life back, or did I? The life I had before had turned into a relentless stream of running. I hardly slept, hardly ate, and had very little time for my wonderful husband and gorgeous family. My aim had been a lifestyle business; I had no life or style, what had gone wrong?

Did I really want to re-create a stressed out life and an unhealthy body with a tortured brain that snatched sleep away in the early hours and replaced it with fear?

It was at this point the anger began to rise. How could I have been so stupid?

I was an educated, sensible person. I came from a wonderfully supportive family and had enjoyed a good education. I was a trained accountant with a background in finance as well as an experienced and well-trained therapist.

The last 13 years had been passionately spent learning about the body and the effect of stress. I knew how the body responded to its environment and how the nurture of mind, body, and spirit led to wellbeing. Why then had I worked so hard, neglected all of my training, and got myself into this mess?

Of course it had happened over time, slowly my enthusiasm had been replaced by fear and I had allowed myself to buy into the plan to just work harder. A few more hours, some extra energy; I had ploughed everything I had into my business and the rest of my life had suffered.

Hindsight is a wonderful thing and I was so cross! I wanted to stomp, shout, moan, and pout about the whole thing; which I did, for a while.

If the universe had wanted me to give in and sit back in my chair, close my shop, and give up on life, then there was one tiny fact it had overlooked: I am stubborn.

As a child, once I had an idea I would make it happen. As a teenager, once I had changed my mind and decided on a new career path there would be no dissuading me. Being born a Pisces meant I would dither, avoid decisions, and sway from one possibility to another. However, once my mind was made up that was it – I would gather my laser focus and make magic happen.

After the despair, the floor sitting and the boiling anger a new feeling began to rise: determination. I could sit and wallow feeling sorry for myself for as long as I liked but this wouldn't change the past.

My choice was obvious, I needed to forgive myself.

I had been brave enough to embark on an adventure, to have a go at creating the business I had dreamed of. Much had gone right, but I had made some mistakes. I had been a human being and made errors, as everyone else did too. Once I truly forgave myself, I could let go of the anger, the fear, and frustration and welcome in more positive emotions.

I didn't want to go backwards and I couldn't change my past, but in my future there were endless possibilities. I could do anything I liked once my strength was back, the world was my oyster!

It wasn't a conscious thought that brought about this change, more a gentle wash of a new emotion; kindness. Each day, I would think about how to be kind to myself and made decisions accordingly. I ate lovely food that would nourish and made sure I always included a good breakfast.

When I was in pain, I took painkillers instead of battling through and made time for holistic therapies that helped the pain permanently disappear.

If I woke up feeling tired and achy, I would get cover and spend a day at home sleeping and reading. I learned to accept the help that had been there all along. Tomorrow was another day and my list would wait.

At last, I let my family lend a hand and they all breathed a sigh of relief! It must have been hard to look on and watch me torturing myself, refusing their help, and love. Once I knew help was on hand, I became more capable anyway and the time when I was at work was focused and productive, as well as fun! I re-discovered the passion and enthusiasm that had started me on this adventure.

With a calm mind and a cared for body, I was able to plan more activities and more people came through the door. We started to build a stable business with routines and a strategy, which was so much better than my previously frantic efforts.

I was able to step away any time I chose and so I no longer felt a slave. We limited our evenings too so I could spend time with my husband and family.

Within the space of three weeks, much had changed. From being on the brink of giving up, hurting, angry, and afraid I now felt supported and loved from the inside out. From a dead ended bolthole I had risen upwards and now once again my future welcomed me.

What had changed? My attitude. I remembered who I was and what I was capable of. Forgiving myself had opened up a whole new, wonderful chapter.

So dear reader, here is my wish for you. I wish you a stubborn streak! A, 'won't give up insisting life could be better,' twist in your character that allows you to be everything you dream of and to enjoy every moment of toe curling happiness that life offers you.

Patricia LeBlanc RM(T)

Patricia LeBlanc is a 5 time International Best Selling Author, Radio/TV/Podcast Host, Abundance/Success Coach, Reiki Master/Teacher, Certified IET™ Master Instructor, Certified Angel Card Reader™, and compiler of the upcoming book, 'Manifesting a New Life: Money, Love, Health and everything in between.' Patricia specializes in strategies to identify powerful breakthroughs to manifest your dream life, while letting go of fears. She takes a holistic approach to helping YOU discover happiness and live a fulfilled life that allows you to remain true to yourself. Download Patricia's free chakra clearing audio at www.patriciaeleblanc.com

You can reach Patricia at:

Website: www.patriciaeleblanc.com

Website: www.patricialeblanc.ca

Website: www.manifestinganewlife.com

Email: info@patricialeblanc.ca

Facebook: www.facebook.com/leblancpatricia

Facebook Page: www.facebook.com/leblancpatricia1

LinkedIn: www.linkedin.com/in/leblancpatricia

Twitter: www.twitter.com/leblancpatricia

Instagram: www.instagram.com/leblancpatricia

Forgiving My Bullies Has Allowed Me to Move Forward in Life

By Patricia LeBlanc RM(T)

"By holding on to what others did to you, you are not harming them, but yourself. Learn to forgive so that you can you move on to be in a better place and have a better life." Patricia LeBlanc, RM(T)

I was blessed to be part of Book 3 of the Missing Piece Series, 'Missing Piece: A Life Transformed,' and so blessed to be part of book 4 about forgiveness. I have several amazing and powerful stories that I could have written about forgiveness, but decided to write about bullying and the effect it has had on me. I chose to write about this after I came out publically about being bullied on my Radio Show, "Motivate and Manifest Success with Patricia." My goal in writing this is to inspire you to learn to let go and forgive as it is very important.

My Story

Growing up, I was a very introverted child. My comfort zone was very limited. When I say very limited, I mean it to the point that the school psychologist told my dad that I must have mental issues and will never accomplish anything in my life as I would not talk to him and my dad replied back that you are not part of her comfort zone therefore she will not talk to you.

I felt like I did not have a voice nor did I fight back. I was very unique and did not fit in. It was easy for others to tease me, call me names or even bully me as I would not take a stand against them. I was teased because I was different from others. I now value being unique and different, but at the time I did not. I became lost and tried to fit in with everything and everyone.

I remember at times, that I wanted to kill myself as I could not take the pain of being bullied anymore. I did not feel loved or even worthy of living. It was hard for me to stand up for myself; I had no voice as I let others take it away from me. I allowed all of this to happen. I carried the effect of this for years and into my twenties, I would numb myself with alcohol and food. I am still amazed that I did not become an alcoholic. I guess my Angels were watching out for me.

It all stopped in Jr high when I had kicked one of the bullies in the butt. He had a hard time sitting as he was in a lot of pain; I really kicked him hard. I took it out on him all the years of being bullied. I had enough and decided to finally start standing up for myself.

In 2004, I did a major depression, which was my wake up call. I started to re-evaluate everything about my life; this was the journey to finally waking up and living my true potential, while being true to myself. I also realized that it was time for me to let go of everything toxic/bad that everyone has ever done to me. It was time for me to forgive not only others, but also myself. I learned to stop giving a damn what others expected of me and to go after my dreams. I became empowered that day!

Was it easy to forgive others including myself? Hell no, but I can tell you it was worth getting out of my comfort zone to do it. I would not be where I am today as host of a successful radio/TV/podcast show, an International Best Seller Several times, or be truly free to be 100% myself and to be making all of my dreams come true. I am not saying this to brag, but to show you that if I was able to learn to forgive my bullies and anyone who has ever did anything bad to me and let it go and become successful, so can you. I am saying this so that I can inspire you because I could have continued being a victim and instead chose to overcome this.

Do I sometime fall back and get angry or hurt about past experiences? Oh hell yes, I am only human. It normally does not last long and I will look at an inspirational quote I keep on my wall:

"Let go of what no longer serves you, learn to forgive others for their past mistakes, learn to forgive yourself of your past mistakes, you deserve to be happy and you need to let go and forgive. If you do not forgive and let go then it will become toxic and drain you and you will not achieve your true potential and therefore will not shine your light to the world. LET GO AND FORGIVE AS YOU DESERVE TO BE HAPPY!"- Patricia LeBlanc

I am grateful that I am alive now and I now know I needed to go through this experience in order to be able to help others to be true to themselves and also shine their light. I am grateful that I have chosen to wake up and to show up in the world.

The importance of Forgiveness

Some people will say that the bullies are 100% responsible, but let me tell you that I was just as responsible as them. I know I will piss off some people, but some school of thought (which I believe in also) is that everything that happens to us is because we attract it on a subconscious level.

Now when someone piss me off or does something to hurt me, I do the following Ho'oponopono cleaning technique, which I repeat either out loud or in my head the following,

"I love you! I am Sorry! Please forgive me! Thank You!"

These four sentences are very powerful. Saying these after a negative experience has allowed me to be able to forgive and let go. It has also helped me with my relationships with people who have done me harm at one time or another, including myself.

I forgave my bullies years ago and I am even connected with a few of them on social media. In the last several years, many bullies have reached out to me to ask me for forgiveness for their behavior towards me during our childhood. I am proud to say that they actually changed for the best and have become better people.

Recently, one of them told me that they were glad that I managed to overcome all of the damage that was inflicted on me during my childhood bullying to be the successful person that I am today. They said that I was a role model as they had hit rock bottom and it made them reflect a lot and knew they needed to reach out and apologize to me.

I have forgiven myself for my role that I played in being bullied and also others.
It is very important to not only forgive others, but to forgive yourself. Forgive others not because it will harm them; you do them no harm in holding on to all that anger. Forgive others because you need to do it for yourself.

How to forgive others and yourself

Here are some tips on how to forgive not only others but yourself:

- Realize that the hate you feel toward others does not harm them in the way that you want, but in fact harms you.
- Understand that the best revenge against others is to live a successful and happy life.
- Make a list of the good things that emerged as a result of this awful experience.
- Be compassionate with yourself.
- Stop telling "the story".
- Retrain your thinking. When their evil actions come to mind, send them a blessing and wish them well.
- Maintain perspective.

If I was able to overcome my childhood bullies and forgive them and myself, then so can you.

I hope that I will be able to inspire at least one person to forgive their bullies or anyone who has harmed them and to learn to let it go once and for all so that they can truly move on with their life. It is your time to be truly happy as you deserve to be. We are all meant to be happy.

Remember the best revenge is to be truly successful and happy; you deserve to be as it is our entire life mission to do so.

If my chapter resonates with you, please do not hesitate to reach out to me. I would love to be able to help you.

Renee Mysliwiec

International Best Selling Published Author and Board Certified Integrative Nutrition Health Coach, Licensed Massage Therapist, mood enlightenment mentor, transition assistant, lover of nature, and most importantly mother of 7 incredible children and "Mammy" to 17 adorable grandchildren!

Renee's story of the heart-breaking end of her 27 year marriage to the love of her life, and what transpired after her husband left, is the basis for her amazing transformational story of forgiveness. She uses her experience to help women through difficult life transitions in their health and business. Through Renee's guidance you'll learn to open up your heart and mind, find clarity, recognize your innate gifts, and be able to see the possibility of a new beautiful *present*, which is your divine birth right.

When working with Renee, you will experience revitalized health, enhanced self-confidence, and liberation. You will learn to dream again and through her techniques in imagery, your soul will be empowered to tap into your greatest form of creation.

Renee's universal work includes:

Coaching

Holistic Therapy

Live Radio Broadcasts

Motivational/Educational Workshops

Speaking Engagements

You can reach Renee at:

Email: renee@healingenergiesinc.com

Facebook: https://www.facebook.com/renee.millermysliwiec

Facebook: https://www.facebook.com/healingenergiesinc

Website: http://www.healingenergiesinc.com/

Website: http://www.healingenergiesinc.com/holistic-living-on-air.html

Website: http://www.wholelifeabundanceinternational.org/home.html

LinkedIn: https://www.linkedin.com/in/healingenergiesinc

Unexpected Loss
By Renee Mysliwiec

In 2008, my husband changed. He began to experience a midlife crisis. Within a year of this change, he decided to leave me and our family. We had been married for 27 years. His leaving led to an unexpected journey for us all.

Almost immediately divorcees began to come out of the woodwork. My husband began dating, even before he had filed for divorce. This was devastating to me. I couldn't understand how he could leave everything we had built together and choose to BE with these women, who didn't seem to care one iota that we were *still married*, that he was contemplating dissolving a *27 year marriage*, or that there were children and grandchildren at home deeply wounded by his decision and missing him terribly.

On one particularly disturbing occasion, my husband had planned to take our younger boys for the evening. I was thrilled for them because it had been several months since their father spent any time with them. To my dismay, I found out that he had intended to take them to a party where there would be drinking. Our younger boys were only 12 and 14. This was a very different lifestyle from the one we had always lived. Their father choosing to do this was a betrayal of everything we had ever taught our children. With my eldest son's help, we intervened and the boys did not go to the party. However, from that point on, any time my husband had the boys, I knew there was a possibility of them being exposed to alcohol, drugs, and promiscuity.

It was completely unnerving for me. I wanted so much to protect my young sons, to influence them in a morally healthy way. I wanted them to grow up healthy, strong, virtuous, and knowing moral boundaries. I felt at their tender ages that they were highly impressionable and I was angry with their father for introducing them to a lifestyle that we had agreed years ago, would not be something we would ever participate in. I knew they needed time with him, so I felt I could not and would not keep them from him. I tried hard to help their dad see what he was doing. I hoped that this would change, to no avail.

During one occasion with their dad, the boys were introduced to several girls. My youngest son became enamoured with one of them. Soon after, I found him and this girl sitting together in my living room. She was sitting on him and kissing his neck. Of course, I put a stop to this and explained our family rules. Also, after hearing them talk about going to the movies together, I reminded my son of our rule; our children do not date until age 16; he was only 12. Immediately this girl said, "Well, that's a stupid rule!" I was fuming. How dare she criticize our rules in my own home! I thought, 'What a disrespectful little brat!'

Not long after this event, I found out they went behind my back, disobeyed our family rules, and chose to go to the movies on a date.

I wanted my son to have nothing to do with her, but of course, that was not his thought.

She was the niece through marriage, of one of the women whom my husband chose to sleep with while we were still married. The woman he eventually lived with, chose to marry, and later divorced; this was the woman whom I would plead with, to help her understand that my children needed time with their father. The woman who basically, spit in my face and told me she didn't care and would do nothing to support me in helping their father see how much his sons and daughters needed him. The woman who ultimately turned my girls against me. The woman who stood in a court room and tried to convince the judge that I was a "stalker" and then watched and testified to try to convince the judge that I was an unfit mother. All this, to try to keep me from seeing my son, or from picking him up at his dad's home on the weekends. This girl was related to the woman who betrayed me over and over again…EVEN when I had done my best to accept the situation, forgive her and I *tried* to be friends!

I did not want my son entangled with this girl or her family. My wounded heart could not stand the idea of them being together. It turned my stomach and literally made me sick. Anger filled my soul whenever I saw her; it brought back all the pain of my loss.

In the fall of 2014, I heard they broke up. I was relieved. This feeling didn't last long. In November my son, now 18, called me from the hospital. This girl had just gotten out of surgery with a tubular pregnancy. It had been scary for him as she had lost a lot of blood and could have died. Her fallopian tube had to be removed. He realized how much he did not want to lose her. My heart softened. I could only imagine going through something like this. I sent my sincere concern and well wishes. I made my son promise that they would be *careful* in the future.

In December, my son decided to move to Wyoming to be with the rest of our family. We were thrilled. I was especially looking forward to having him live with me. I had high hopes of finally being able to spend time with him and make up for the loss of not being able to raise him for several years while he lived with his father. In February, he came home to us. To my dismay, they were together again, and *she* decided to come to Wyoming too!

Shortly thereafter at a family dinner, he announced his girlfriend was pregnant. I struggled with this. If he were to marry this girl, we would be forever connected to the, "other women", the woman who had become my mortal enemy *and* her sister-in-law. How could I ever handle this?

I plead with God, "Why are you doing this to me? I have prayed for my son to find another girl. Couldn't you give me this one request? Must I really be forever connected to the women who have caused me so much pain?"

Through my tears, I poured out my feelings to my son. I asked him to give me time; I would work through this and somehow find a way to be ok. I knew I needed to find a way to love this girl. *I had a grandchild coming!* How could I do it? How could I work through this?

After many tears and weeks of working on my own, through my pain, sorrow, and old memories, I invited his girlfriend to my home to talk. I bought Chinese food and we sat down together.

To my surprise, before I could convey any of my feelings, she expressed her love for my son, and her excitement at starting a family with him. She voiced her desire to love me, and be close to me, her desire to be a part of our family, and her hope in being accepted.

Her words caused me to look at her with *new* eyes.

Our conversation lasted 5 ½ hours. Years of built up pain and deep sorrow poured out. Finally, able to share my feelings with someone connected to this pain felt so good. My son's girlfriend completely validated my feelings; apologizing for the hurt caused by her family and acknowledging the things that had been wrong. She showed complete compassion for my broken heart.

I felt my wall come down and my heart soften. I was surprised as I actually began to feel love for her and sympathy for how she was raised. I felt compassion as she shared the suffering and abuse she experienced in her childhood. This enabled me to release her and begin the healing.

A few weeks later, I noticed that my pants were very loose. *The scale showed 15 whole pounds lost!!* I had been eating a healthy diet for years, but had not been able to lose weight. Now it was falling off of me!

Because of the intense grief, my body had held on to the weight. When she and my son listened to me and validated my feelings, along with giving *myself* permission to speak my words and honor my true emotions, this shift was able to take place; the emotions *and fat* were released from the cells of my body.

Unexpectedly, who her family is was no longer important.

She comes from a different background. At times, she is loud and boisterous, but I can honestly say that my heart has been able to open up. I *now* appreciate her beautiful qualities. I *now* truly love her. Forgiveness has come!

Richelle Traversano

Richelle Traversano is an International Best-selling Author and writer and is a motorcycle and life enthusiast. Her various non-fiction book collaborations are excellent examples that, with tenacity and a change of perspective, you can overcome and conquer obstacles in your life. Richelle is embarking on a journey of fiction writing and poetry series this year and is a firm believer in copious amounts of laughter, good books, and chocolate. She is learning to navigate through the world since the loss of her Mother, and will hug you tighter and longer than sometimes necessary. Richelle is a proud Canadian, but prefers American pricing.

You can reach Richelle at:

Website: www.richellewrites.com

Email: richelleauthoress@gmail.com

Facebook: www.facebook.com/richelle.traversano

Instagram: www.instagram.com/richellechucklesgiggles

Twitter Handle: @chucklesgiggles

The Art of Forgiveness
By Richelle Traversano

There have been times in my life when forgiving someone or forgiving the nature of a situation was essential to my health and wellness. Though I did not agree with what was said or done in certain circumstances, it freed me from the devastating effects of toxic emotions and anger. Even those times when forgiveness didn't seem possible because of the severity of harm or the anguish incurred, it was the only solution for me in order to move forward. In doing this, I learned that forgiveness is first and foremost a healthy choice; a personal and a vital one.

But what happens when the imperative action of forgiveness lies not in giving it to someone or something else, but rather, in gifting forgiveness to yourself? That question took me on a soul searching mission, a journey through grief's gut wrenching and life changing fury.

In the spring of 2009, just nine days before my thirty-fourth birthday, my mother passed away unexpectedly. My mom was my best friend. I adored her. I admired her capacity for having an open, loving, and giving nature. Without a doubt, she was the most beautiful piece of my heart. When the reality struck me that there would never be another chance to see, talk, or experience the rest of my life with her, I came undone; completely and entirely unravelled.

There was no last, 'good-bye', no last, 'I love you', no last mom-hug. No more coffees, laughs, lunches or dinners, no more special occasions and shared moments; she was just...gone. The agonizing, sombre realization that I didn't get a chance to say all

174

the things I should have said, or do all the things I should have done, that I didn't take opportunities to right any wrongs or take advantage of every moment I had with her, left me drowning in a deep sea of misery and regret. Days upon months upon years of feeling utter sadness and grief. Loss is an inevitable darkness that I wish upon no one, but it is a lugubrious fact of life, one that a great deal of us has experienced or will at some point.

Grief and its unwelcome reality were unapologetic and relentless. It was a harsh reminder of moments left frozen in time.

The first two years without her felt like the world was moving and changing at a rapid pace, while I stood frozen in my tracks. My mind was locked in slow motion playback of all the things I should have done differently when she was here. I replayed all of my hopes and dreams for her, for us, and for everyone in the family, that never came to fruition. That caused me extreme sorrow.

The despair I felt in her absence was something that I thought I deserved. I was painstakingly furious with myself for not being the best version of me when she was here.

Even though there was an abundance of happy memories, years of words and wisdom, and an enormous amount of love she left behind, it was difficult to make sense of, or draw strength from the positive when I was beating myself up emotionally with the negative. I falsely believed that I deserved to feel awful and guilty because I was here and she wasn't. I couldn't comprehend how that was even possible.

The next couple of years were a learning curve. I made my way through some of the darkest days and nights in my life. I did everything and yet, I did nothing at the same time.

I thought I was on the right path when I decided to take control of my grief and work with it instead of against it. Self-improvement was, in my mind, a sure fire way to stitch together the shattered pieces of me. I became active, I joined a gym and I lost an incredible amount of weight. Healthy? Yes. Problem solved? No. Because I put so much time and effort into one aspect of the ruins of my circumstance, I neglected other areas in my life. One step forward two steps back. I continued to waltz to that tune for a very long time, but something had to give.

THE SIX YEAR ACHE

There is something to be said for perseverance. Even in my darkest hours, something in the depths of me knew that I would keep going. I was, and am, determined to live this life, not just exist in it. I know that I am fortunate to be here.

But being hard on myself had become second nature. There was still a missing piece that I had yet to grasp.

Not wanting to give into the grief without a fair attempt at coercing it into co-operative submission, I learned to chalk up the baby steps, the small wins, as victories. In the grand scheme of things, these were the stepping stones of the journey. I celebrated the occasions when getting out of bed took more strength than a strong man pulling a bus with teeth would, but I managed it. In turn, I was gentle on myself when opening up the front door to breathe fresh air into my weary soul, was as much as I could do for that day.

However, setbacks still occurred. I would get angry at myself any time frustrations fell out of my mouth or patience was not on my side with people, places or things. When laughter would escape me, or a smile appeared on my lips, unforced, I didn't feel worthy. If I enjoyed a moment or a feel good emotion, I felt guilty. I was neck deep in trial and error learning how to navigate through this world without my mom.

I knew that no amount of wishing, hoping, or deal making would bring her back. Words left unsaid would be just that. I could not relive moments with her and make them better, make them more, make them last. I had to face the stark truth that all I could do was start to make the most of today and each day after that.

She was my real life super hero for as long as, and as far back as I can remember. I wish I could have saved her life that fateful night and come to her rescue to be her super hero too.

It ate away at the very core of my being that my mom, my best friend in life, the one who gave me so much and asked for so little, was gone. No matter how much I loved her, was it enough? Did she know the depths of joy she brought to my life? She told me during our last Christmas together that her wish for me was to be happy. I wanted to honor her request, but how?

One answer. One word.

Forgiveness.

Just as easy and as hard as that.

Up to this point I was proficient in avoiding the remedy because I thought it meant letting her go. I was wrong. Removing the heavy weight of guilt and sorrow from my thoughts and forgiving myself only brought her closer to me in ways I never expected. I understood so much more about her as my mother and as a woman. In turn, I learned more about me as a daughter and a woman too. Now I have an even bigger appreciation and deep gratitude for the unique dynamic that was our powerful mother/daughter/best-friend relationship. Forgiveness offered my heart, mind, and soul acceptance instead of resistance.

Forgiving is an unadulterated act of courage. It doesn't excuse behavior; it makes you take responsibility for your well-being. I still wander the scenic route of grief's unmerciful experience; I am not immune to the sadness and loneliness that comes from not having my mother here. I am, however, better equipped to be gentler with my thoughts and actions.

The passage through the ebb and flow of grief is a profound and personal experience. Grief and loss is inevitable, but love and hope are too.

This journey has been difficult; it has brought me to my knees more often than not. It has also made me grow. I miss my mom with a force of nature so great that it cannot be measured in weight, only infinite love. The little girl in me will always be a little lost without her mom. The woman in me will always be a little lost too, but I know enough now to seize every day and to appreciate all that is and all that was. I will always carry with me the precious time we shared.

My experience has taught me that forgiveness is an offering of peace to one's self. I have become intimate with its themes and lessons.

If ever need be, I hope you never deny yourself the messy and beautiful anguishing art of forgiveness.

Toni Idiaquez

Toni spent 30 years discovering and practicing Mind, Body, and Spirit medicine. She has discovered that the root of anxiety is fear, which are often times brought about by a previous trauma. She is the Author of the upcoming book, 'You Can't Tell By Looking: Overcoming The Battlefield of PTSD.'

Toni holds a Master's Degree in Oriental Medicine, practices energy medicine, walks the Red Road (Native American Spirituality), and follows Indigenous ways. She works with clients in a way that addresses the Spiritual root, as well as the physical dimensions to bring about healing. She found in her own life and her clients' the importance and freedom that true forgiveness brings.

Toni is creating retreats that will teach people how to find and resolve the root issue that is limiting their ability to live their life fully so they can create the life they want all the way around.

Toni is the founder of, 'ASA Wellness Center' and, 'New Life 360'.

You can reach Toni at:

Website: www.newlife360.com

Freedom That Forgiveness Brings
By Toni Idiaquez

"The most exquisite act one can do for one self is to forgive."

~Toni Idiaquez

Definition of Forgiveness is to cease to feel resentment against another who has done you wrong.

I personally found much lightness and freedom when I truly and fully forgave. There are two very distinct times I remember forgiving someone; although there are many times I have forgiven others. One of the times I didn't even realize I was holding resentment and anger against this person or that I had forgiven him until I forgave another. This individual I will call John. The other person I forgave was deliberate. I will call this person David. (I have changed their names to protect their identity).

John and I grew up together from 4th grade through high school. Throughout junior high, John would pick on me and tease me. Now, I never bought into the idea that he teased me because he liked me as my mother would tell me. I also didn't understand the notion that boys pull girls ponytails as a way of affection. I felt that part of the reason was that on one of the occasions during high school when John was picking on me that my feelings were hurt. Well, I told my mom. Wrong thing to do! What my mother said to me etched in my brain forever, "Toni, go get the bicycle chain out of the storage shed and take it to school and beat the shit out of John and if the Principle says anything to you, tell him to call me." Now, talk about confusion, we were raised, or so I thought, to be nice, not to hit, help people, and stick up for the underdog. My parents were both like that. The well-intentioned communication of standing up for yourself without being told was confusing to say the least, especially since it was communicated in that way. Historically, my mother stood up for her younger brother by, "beating the shit out of the older boys who picked on him." Needless to say, that worked for her and ceased the bullies from bulling her little brother.

Let's fast forward to the moment in time that the forgiveness happened for me with John, some 12 years later. I'm in for a visit and attending a little league basketball game that my nephew is playing and John's son is on my nephew's team. I go over and sit by John to catch up, as I hadn't seen him since a year or two after we left high school. I discovered that his massage therapist was my old roommate, and he just adored her, so we had common ground. Through our conversation I also found out that he served in the Army, as did I. He made the rank of Sergeant, another commonality. What John shared with me about his experience in the Army and what he learned about himself created the space for me to forgive. All of a sudden it was like a weight was lifted off of me that I didn't even know existed. I felt lighter and free. All of a sudden it was gone, the feeling I felt about him, what I thought about him as a person. I had no idea that I carried around resentment toward John.

John shared with me that his troops didn't respect him. They wouldn't do what he would tell them to do! Now, in the military you are supposed to do what a higher-ranking person tells you to do, period. When he finally gained insight into the why, that he was an Asshole, pushy, egotistical…just as he was through grade school and high school, he did an about face and turned around.

It showed up as respecting his fellow soldiers, kindness, working with them, and actually caring about these soldiers and their families. Just that mere conversation and John sharing his lesson, created the space for the instant decision of forgiveness to take place. In fact, I didn't even realize that what I did was forgiveness until the time that I decided to consciously forgive my ex-husband David.

Being in love and planning to spend the rest of our lives together was what I thought was going to happen when we had married.

Well, it didn't turn out that way, the heat turned up. David came into my life to be a, "Gift", and he was and still is. I adore this man and love him more now than ever. You see, I prayed to Spirit that I wanted to be nothing less than unconditionally loving, to have healthy relationships, and to have no more drama in my life. The saying, "be careful of what you ask for or you just might get it," came true, but not like I thought.

I was gifted with a healing of my life through this relationship. David showed me areas where I didn't love myself, where I lived in drama, and didn't have healthy relationships with men due to the death of my father. Also, I believe I was able to forgive David and myself because a couple of months before the incident that led to me ending the relationship, I had the worst day of my life.

The worst day of my life was when I fully came to realize I was angry with Spirit. Who me? I was always seeking the Truth, seeking Spirit, to be in alignment, advising others to trust Spirit! Here I was not trusting Spirit, shut off from the fullest connection with Spirit, and myself. Three days before the worst day of my life, I was in a session with my Trauma Counsellor and she recognized from one statement I had made, "my dad was reading the Bible the day before he offed himself", that I was mad at Spirit. I didn't have any emotion when I said it and I never felt like I was mad at HIM! However, we went through the sequence and techniques she uses and then I went home. On the third day (funny how this is Easter Day when I am writing this) what lay in the subconscious was brought to the surface after the techniques my counsellor used. I never felt more tortured and heartbroken than that day. It took me until 2pm to get dressed as I went from being ok to feeling tortured, balling my eyes out, over and over again. As my mother often told us, "this too shall pass", and it did! The very act of getting over being mad at Spirit for the death of my father, allowed me to forgive my father and my ex-partner.

The New Year was upon us and David was out of town doing business, again. I wasn't invited and that hurt because he was in Spain, a country in which my father's lineage is from. This led to many arguments and I wasn't feeling loved. While he was on business we spoke a couple of times and there seemed to be a disconnect between us, something felt off.

Spirit had been urging me to take my business back, to get his hand out of my pocket, and set boundaries. David had been self-employed his whole life and when I married him he seemed to be successful; he had significant debt, but he owned a couple of commercial buildings among other projects. He was always involving himself in a new project. To me he was the busiest non-productive person I knew. It would be different if he had been contributing to the family in the least little way. I asked him to get a job, something, just to ease the burden on me financially and emotionally, but he threw a fit like a spoiled child. One day out of frustration, I asked him what he would do if I wasn't covering the bills, covering him. He responded that he could make something happen! Imagine that, the man I married would only do something if he had too! A light went off.

I was hearing Spirit more clearly when I felt disconnected from David, my intuition said to take a look all of my accounts. This was also a time of taxes and David called me over to sign them. I knew I had been working a lot, but didn't pay close attention to how much I actually collected. I discovered that I earned six figures that year. Well, great right. I also discovered I was 30 K in Credit Card debt. I realized I had my head in the sand; I wanted what was promised, a marriage with a family. That I didn't receive. No children, no sex, no husband, just a child being a kept man. The whole marriage was a farce, so he could look successful. I was used to the extreme! The lease on the house was ending and I found a place to live. I told David that the marriage was over, he could go find a place to live and do what it would take to make it on his own. David had no job because mama (me) was taking care of everything. The man deliberately took from me under the pretence of marriage and faith (Christian faith). I broke free and now had to rebuild my life. The decision to kick a man out in the street without a dime was the hardest thing I have ever done, but I had no choice if I was going to live. In order to live fully and thrive I had to forgive David or it would eat me alive.

What did it take for me to forgive David? I made a deliberate conscious decision to forgive him for any pain he had unconsciously or consciously caused me, this included the farce of a marriage, among other painful moments and events. I also told him that I hoped he could forgive me for any pain that I may have caused him.

The forgiveness with David is so complete that I have to remind myself of what happened. I am so free that my love is greater and more complete than ever before. I sit in amazement of the lightness and freedom that complete forgiveness has brought to me. I am in gratitude!

Conclusion

Am I glad that I swallowed my ego and faced my fears of stepping up and leading this book project and growing it into a publishing company? You bet I am because here we are today with a 4th book and compilers contributing their own books in the series.

Life presents us with some huge scary moments and it is up to us to either move forward or stay stuck where we are. To move forward we have to become aware by taking responsibility for who we are now, so that we can become who we want to be.

The people within these pages have shared their amazing stories of courage and scary moments they had to face in hope to make you see that forgiveness is the way forward and to help you become free from the pain you are experiencing. This is not just to forgive others, but mostly to ourselves so we no longer have to live with the horrible bitter emotions that go with it.

Along 'The Missing Piece' book journey, every book subject has resonated with exactly where Emily and I have come to in our journeys. To have people join us from all over the world and stand with us to share their stories on the same subjects has really inspired me to keep going. Something that started out so painful for us became a global movement of inspiration.

I want to leave this conclusion by sharing with you that I am so deeply honored and humbled to be the leader of 'The Missing Piece'. I am also really happy to share with you that Emily has now grown into one amazing strong women who is happy, stress free, about to become a mother, and is carrying her first child.

As she laid in bed with me watching movies one evening she looked at me and said "If I have a girl I am calling her after you mum".

Next year I could very well have a granddaughter named, **August Katy Emily Marsh.** She will be named after my month of birth and followed by my first and second name.

I want to you to know that forgiveness brought me to this amazing legacy. It can bring you here too!

Kate Gardner

#1 International Best-Selling Author/International Success Coach & CEO and creator of The Missing Piece Publishing House.

Invites you to compile your very own book in International Best-Selling Book Series. We pay YOU to become a published author and have every intention of taking you to the best-sellers list!

For more information please visit

www.themissingpiecebooks.com

This not the end, it is JUST the beginning ☺